Bruckner Remembered

Stephen Johnson was born in Lancashire in 1955. As a teenager he tried composing: mostly symphonies for vast forces, and a concerto for five saxophones and orchestra. Studies with Alexander Goehr at Leeds University encouraged him to think more realistically. After a short period at the BBC Gramophone Library, he continued his musical studies at Manchester University with Ian Kemp, researching the cultural and political background to the music of Shostakovich. In 1984, two friends – the composer Robert Simpson and the record producer Andrew Keener – suggested he try musical journalism. This soon developed into a full-time career. Since then, he has contributed regularly to *The Independent* and *Gramophone* magazine, and has broadcast frequently on BBC Radio 3, Radio 4 and the World Service. His most extensive broadcast project was a series of fourteen programmes for Radio 3 about the symphonies of Bruckner for the composer's centenary year. He is married and lives in London.

in the same series

BARTOK REMEMBERED
by Malcolm Gillies

DEBUSSY REMEMBERED
by Roger Nichols

GERSHWIN REMEMBERED
by Edward Jablonski

MAHLER REMEMBERED
by Norman Lebrecht

MENDELSSOHN REMEMBERED
by Roger Nichols

PURCELL REMEMBERED
by Michael Burden

RAVEL REMEMBERED
by Roger Nichols

SATIE REMEMBERED
by Robert Orledge

SHOSTAKOVICH: A LIFE REMEMBERED
by Elizabeth Wilson

TCHAIKOVSKY REMEMBERED
by David Brown

BRUCKNER REMEMBERED

STEPHEN JOHNSON

faber and faber

LONDON · BOSTON

First published in 1998
by Faber and Faber Limited
3 Queen Square London WC1N 3AU

Phototypeset by Intype London Ltd
Printed in England by Clays Ltd, St Ives plc

A CIP record for this book
is available from the British Library

ISBN 0-571-17095-1

2 4 6 8 10 9 7 5 3 1

For Kate

CONTENTS

LIST OF ILLUSTRATIONS

For permission to reproduce illustrations the author and publisher are grateful to the British Library (7, 9, 10, 11, 12, 14, 17 – from *Anton Bruckner*, August Göllerich/Max Auer); Gesellschaft der Musikfreunde in Wien (1, 2, 4, 5, 6, 8, 13, 15, 16, 19).

INTRODUCTION

It is generally said that Bruckner was a very simple man – practically a nature boy, you would gather from some writers. If, after listening to one of his symphonies, you still think that he was simple, then you are not the kind of person who should be reading this book.

That rare flash of insight occurs in *The Bluffer's Guide to Music* (London, 1985, p. 33). Eleven years after that provocative little book first appeared, and a century after the composer's death, Bruckner is still widely regarded as an inspired simpleton. Ken Russell's television film, *The Strange Affliction of Anton Bruckner* (1990), portrayed the composer as a kind of visionary idiot: a man through whom music flowed directly from the divine source, with virtually no intellectual mediation. That may be an extreme view, but it is based on a long-established tradition, one that began in Bruckner's own lifetime. Several of the writers in this collection appear to confirm it. For Linda Schönbeck (p. 19), Bruckner was 'a child of nature [*ein Naturkind*] – innocent, naïve, without malice'. Fritz Kreisler (p. 26) describes him as 'a man without guile and of a childlike naïvety. He had two co-ordinates – music and religion. Beyond that he knew almost nothing. I doubt whether he could even multiply or subtract correctly.' Describing one of Bruckner's notoriously frequent infatuations with young girls, Friedrich Klose (p. 52) suggests that 'her enchanting, unspoilt quality spoke to something in his own childlike nature'.

Could this Bruckner really be the same individual who produced those complex and original symphonies, or the great church works? Richard Capell, writing in the old Pelican book, *The Symphony* (1949), evidently thought so. He offers a typical explanation: Bruckner arrived at his now widely admired musical structures 'By instinct if not by design' (p. 220). But, like most English-speaking commentators, Capell has nothing to say about the nature of this remarkable instinct, or about how it might be consistent with the notion of a 'simple' mind. I began my researches for this book in the hope that at least one or two of those who remembered Bruckner would be able to throw light on this – to take us beyond the image of the 'inspired Simpleton'. Some patience was needed, but eventually I was rewarded. There are insights into a much more complicated, sometimes tormented soul. Alexander Fränkel (p. 35–6) recalls Bruckner's lively (if unpolished) intelligence and intellectual curiosity. Others offer glimpses of a Bruckner who could be stimulating company: funny, self-mocking, even witty. Then there is Carl Hruby's astonishing revelation (p. 33) that Bruckner had read *Das Leben Jesu* ('The Life of Jesus') by the nineteenth-century liberal theologian David Strauss, and that he was prepared to admit to a 'speculative' element in his own Catholic faith: 'if it's true, so much the better for me; if it isn't true, then praying won't do me any harm'. Richard Heller, in his moving account of Bruckner's final months (pp. 171–7), also detects an ironic, ambiguous note in Bruckner's devotions. Max von Oberleithner and Karl Waldeck have plenty to say about Bruckner's neurotic obsessions and about the terrible nervous breakdown of 1866–7 – interestingly, both of them connect the *Kyrie* from the F minor Mass with this crisis; Oberleithner (pp. 65–6) tells us that composing this movement was a vital stage in Bruckner's subsequent recovery. Waldeck's account is especially poignant, not least because it suggests that humane understanding was all too rare in Bruckner's experience:

> In company, his condition usually led to general merriment, but I felt sorry for him and stayed with him as much as possible, and when I came to take my leave of him late into the night he would beg me to stay, for if he was left to himself he would be tormented by his obsessions again. (p. 46)

An intelligent, sensitive introvert, prey to dark obsessions and, at least in later life, religious doubts – if this is the 'true' Bruckner, how could he have been so widely misunderstood? It's easy to see how Bruckner's gaucheness, gullibility, his lack of social polish, bizarre dress sense, and unselfconscious retention of his Upper Austrian dialect and bluntness of expression would have made him a target of mockery in late nineteenth-century Vienna. This was a very literary culture, heavy with what Henry James called 'the social drapery commonly muffling, in an overcivilized age, the sharpness of human contacts'. Inevitably, Bruckner would stand out in such a society, and his apparent lack of interest in literature would naturally lead to dismissal by some intellectuals – see, for instance, Friedrich Eckstein on Bruckner's relations with Hugo Wolf (p. 142–4). But Eckstein also tells us that Bruckner was widely regarded as a leading musical theorist, which suggests at least some kind of intellectual aptitude. It is also worth mentioning at this point that Bruckner passed his teacher-training exams the first time (not a common achievement), with distinction, and, as Karl Seiberl informs us (p. 14), he also studied Latin and Law – so much for Kreisler's assertion that Bruckner knew nothing beyond music and religion, and for his conjecture that the composer could not 'multiply or subtract correctly'. The idea that Bruckner was a simple-minded, illiterate provincial takes a bit of a knock – especially when you consider that Bruckner also seems to have been regarded as unusual in his Upper Austrian homeland (see the accounts of Linda Schönbeck [pp. 19–22] and Ferdinand Krackowizer [p. 17]).

There could be another reason why so many people got Bruckner wrong. Carl Hruby provides a clue. He quotes the composer on his early years: 'Ten hours a day at the piano, three hours at the organ – that was my daily regime; any time left over was for – recovering.' Hruby tells us that Bruckner said this 'with grim irony'. Karl Waldeck records a very similar remark, and adds that Bruckner's theoretical studies 'would then last well into the night' (p. 45). If anything, Bruckner's regime intensified during his Linz years (1856–68). There were exhaustive (and exhausting) studies with the eminent theorist Simon Sechter (whom Schubert had approached for counterpoint lessons in the last weeks of his life). Extra private studies in Latin and Law have already been mentioned, and there is evidence that Bruckner also looked at physics.

So perhaps Bruckner's social maladroitness stemmed more from his tendency to bury himself in his studies. Academic institutions contain many such characters: obsessive, unworldly, sometimes weirdly eccentric – the stuff of countless student anecdotes. Anyone who has been to music college will recognize the type: it tends to be commonest amongst keyboard players, for whom practice is an especially solitary business, and particularly amongst organists (the isolation of the organ loft). The dedicated keyboard player spends much of his or her time focusing on what sportsmen call the 'inner game', possibly at the expense of the outer, social one.

We now seem to be moving towards a conventional romantic explanation: that Bruckner's eccentricity and *gaucherie* were the price of his dedication to his art. But some of Bruckner's contemporaries hint at other motivations for his compulsion to work: a desire for social self-improvement, or possibly something closer to medieval self-mortification. Max von Oberleithner mentions an unnamed cleric at the monastery of St Florian, where the teenage Bruckner lived and had his first serious education. Apparently this priest advised the young Bruckner that if he wanted to be a composer, he should 'keep himself apart from women'; and in a strange way Bruckner seems to have taken that to heart. The impossibility and rapid transience of most of his infatuations suggest that – perhaps like Beethoven – Bruckner found it more convenient to fall for the unattainable. Several writers, including Friedrich Klose (see above), see something essentially childlike, innocent, in Bruckner's susceptibility to young girls. But Oberleithner (pp. 64–7) portrays a Bruckner tormented by sexual frustration, and cites this as one of the major influences in the crisis of 1866–7. The psychological dynamics were obviously very complicated. Nevertheless, Oberleithner's remarks about the conception of the *Kyrie* from the F minor Mass do seem to confirm the classic Freudian explanation of the urge to create, strikingly anticipated by the poet Heinrich Heine in his *Schöpfungslieder* ('Songs of Creation'):

Krankheit ist wohl der letzte Grund
Des ganzen Schöpferdrangs gewesen;
Erschaffend konte ich genesen,
Erschaffend wurde ich gesund.

('Sickness was in fact the ultimate reason for the whole creative impulse; by creating I was able to recover, by creating I became well.')

Overwork, rigorous devotion to art and to mastering its techniques may have exacerbated Bruckner's obsessional tendencies, especially during the 1866–7 breakdown. But at the same time it seems to have been art that helped him find his way through these mental thickets. And as Anthony Storr says in his classic study *The Dynamics of Creation*, obsessional traits can have a positive function in human creativity: Storr cites Dickens, Swift, Dr Johnson, Ibsen, Stravinsky, Rossini and Beethoven as examples (p. 122). Bruckner's obsessive numbering of every single bar in his manuscripts (most commonly in groups of four, eight or twelve bars) is often put down as a neurotic symptom, a kind of pointless mental 'tic'. Jamie James, in his *Music of the Spheres* (p. 203–4), goes so far as to state that in Bruckner in particular 'we feel intuitively that what we are hearing is the supremely artistic working out of the composer's own neuroses'.* But there is a powerful, if controversial, Freudian school of thought which insists that 'working out of neuroses' is at the root of *all* artistic creation.** And, significantly, Bruckner's counting of bars was not restricted to his own works; he also numbered bars in scores he admired: Mozart's *Requiem*, Beethoven's *Eroica* Symphony. One has only to look at these scores to see that this is not simply a manifestation of compulsive neurosis, rather a detailed periodic analysis of these masterworks, accompanied by equally thorough harmonic analyses (the kind of thing described in this book by several of the composer's students). Bruckner is clearly *consciously* exploring musical proportion. It makes perfect sense: could that extraordinary feeling for architecture, felt by so many Bruckner-lovers, really have been the result of pure instinct, a kind of musical somnambulism? The balance between this and a genuinely debilitating obsessiveness was obviously precarious (see, for instance, Oberleithner on the revision of the First Symphony

*James contrasts Bruckner with Mozart, in whose *Jupiter* Symphony 'we are hearing the turning of the crystal spheres from the celestial point of view'. This is dangerously subjective. I am sure I am not the only listener who has sensed something like the turning of a celestial sphere in the coda of Bruckner's Fourth Symphony, to take just one example; Robert Simpson's *The Essence of Bruckner* makes use of several striking astronomical analogies.

**The idea that instinctual urges can be 'sublimated' in art is not Freud's invention. It is anticipated by Schopenhauer and, most strikingly, by Nietzsche. Anthony Storr revises the Freudian doctrine somewhat in *The Dynamics of Creation*. For Storr, sublimation is an element in human creativity, but the ultimate aim, conscious or not, is the healing of 'internal divisions': 'Man is a creature inescapably, and often unhappily divided; and the divisions within him recurrently impel the use of his imagination to make new syntheses. The creative consequence of his imaginative strivings may never make him whole; but they constitute his deepest consolations and his greatest glories.' (pp. 295–6) *Pace* Jamie James, I would argue that Storr's conclusion is as appropriate to Mozart as it is to Bruckner.

[p. 103]). But how interesting, how urgent would Bruckner's creations have been if it had been less so?

All of this raises another big question: with so many views of Bruckner, some subtly different, some sharply contradictory, whose accounts should we trust? Must the answer be everyone and no one? Readers will form their own opinions, no doubt; but some remarks in Alan Bennett's *Writing Home* (Faber, 1994, p. 148) helped crystallize my own intuitions:

> Those best at saying what they mean aren't always best at meaning what they say . . . I am reading Ryszard Kapuscinski's *The Emperor*, the story of the last days of Haile Selassie. The accounts by the lowliest of the palace officials are the most interesting. Something of Oliver Sacks in the other 'verbatim' accounts. It's not always easy to believe these articulate and over-literary witnesses, or to trust that words are not being put into their mouths.

Reading some of the less literary memoirs, one often feels that the writer is simply keen to get his or her recollections down as they come to mind; their very untidiness or incompleteness makes them the more convincing. Others may be better stylists, but one cannot help wondering whether the author was able to resist the temptation to be artistic, to fill in gaps or tidy up loose ends. The reminiscences of Friedrich Eckstein and Friedrich Klose are particularly polished, each anecdote followed through to its logical conclusion; but when it comes to long chunks of reported dialogue, there has to be an element of invention. This applies to tone as much as to content. (Do some of the more sophisticated Viennese writers exaggerate Bruckner's Upper Austrian dialect?) And yet Carl Hruby mentions notes made soon after conversations or events, and Klose's almost Dickensian eye for detail is one of the things that makes his accounts so fascinating: his description of Bruckner's living quarters (pp. 42–5) is irresistible.

Other reminiscences are suspect for more concrete reasons; interestingly, the ones that worried me most were the last to be written down. Fritz Kreisler's stories were apparently dictated in the late 1940s. I have already given my reasons for doubting Kreisler's remarks about Bruckner's education, and the anecdote about the dog, wonderful though it is, is also problematical (see p. 27 *fn*). Alma Mahler's *Gustav Mahler: Erinnerungen und Briefe* ('Gustav Mahler: Memories and Letters') first appeared in 1940. Her account of Bruckner's engagement to the unnamed chambermaid in Berlin (p. 62) conflicts strikingly with Max von Oberleithner's version of the Berlin trip (pp. 63–8), published seven years earlier. Oberleithner's account is first-hand, Alma Mahler's is not. In Alma's version of the glorious bath-tub story (p. 61), we are told that the unfortunate woman was the mother of the composer Hans Rott; but Rott's mother died when he was just two years old, long before this incident is alleged to have taken place. Obviously there was some embroidery there.

But *Bruckner Remembered* is also about *how* Bruckner was remembered. Some myth-making is inevitable. Other versions of the bath-tub incident had appeared in print by the time Alma Mahler came to write *Erinnerungen und Briefe*. Alexander Fränkel, a friend of the composer, tells us that when the weather was particularly hot, Bruckner would compose in his room, 'stark naked apart from a pair of swimming trunks', and that when the heat became intolerable, he 'stuck his head under the water-tap, and thus refreshed, returned to work' (Göllerich/Auer, *Anton Bruckner. Ein Lebens- und Schaffensbild*, Vol. 4, Band 2, p. 28). It is not hard to see how this could have been gradually elaborated into Alma Mahler's version. This is not to say that Alma Mahler or Kreisler were being wilfully dishonest; but as memories can help in the creation of a myth, so myth can influence the way someone or something is remembered. A story recounted by somebody else can eventually become one's own personal memory, and there is scientific evidence that when we retell a story, we remember it in the form we last told it, not as we originally experienced it. And the Bruckner myth evidently still has the power to *create* stories. On 25 March 1986, BBC Radio 3's magazine programme *Music Weekly* broadcast a short talk, 'A Composer on the Footplate', apparently based on a recollection by one of Bruckner's friends, which claimed that the composer had been a passionate train-spotter, and that several passages in his symphonies were inspired by the sound of steam engines. This turned out to be a spoof, but I am astonished how many people have repeated it to me as though it were established fact. As with so many classic anecdotes, the principle appears to be: *Si non e vero, e ben trovato* – 'If it isn't true, it ought to be'.

Differences in perspective, even outright contradictions, are to be expected in a collection like this; but they can add to the interest, even the value of the book. Friedrich Eckstein and Friedrich Klose disagree profoundly about Bruckner's ability as a teacher; Carl Hruby and Ernst Decsey have strikingly different opinions on some of Bruckner's pupils and their legacy as editors, performers and general champions of the music. Taken together, these contrasting accounts may be felt to add up to a more three-dimensional portrait. It is not difficult to see how these writers might conscientiously have arrived at opposite conclusions.

There is bound to be some disagreement amongst readers as to the value of this book in relation to the music. If one takes the view that a work of art is self-sufficient, to be judged and appreciated without reference to anything outside itself, then *Bruckner Remembered* is likely to be of limited interest. But for this writer/translator, there were many helpful insights into particular works, and into how they were composed. Several writers stress the influence of Sechter's theories on Bruckner's harmonic thinking – though not all of them see that influence as a force for good. Max von Oberleithner's account of how the theme of the finale of the Fourth Symphony came into being (pp. 15–16) is intriguing, not least because it implies an extra-musical explanation as to why the main, unison theme of that movement remains the same in all three versions – though, I admit, Oberleithner is not ideally clear about which theme he means. Carl Hruby tells a lovely story about one of Bruckner's would-be *amours*, and about how he seems to have got her out of his system by playing through the Adagio of the Eighth Symphony (p. 60). The first theme of that movement combines a leading motif from Schubert's melancholy *Der Wanderer* (the motif on which Schubert's *Wanderer* Fantasy is based) with a version of the distinctive syncopated rhythm from Act Two of Wagner's *Tristan und Isolde*; in *Tristan* it introduces the words 'O sink' hernieder, Nacht der Liebe' ('O sink down upon us, night of love'). Is this music really as 'unworldly' as some writers (including Friedrich Eckstein) have suggested? This sort of thing makes one think harder about certain other apparent references in Bruckner: the Wagner quotations in the 1873 version of the first movement of the Third Symphony, for instance. Bruckner quotes the 'Liebestod' motif from *Tristan* and Brunhilde's dissolving 'Sleep' harmonies from *Die Walküre* – both images of women metaphorically or literally falling asleep. Does this have any bearing on Bruckner's remark that part of the Symphony was written in memory of his beloved mother? The 1876 version of the Third Symphony's Adagio combines themes from *Tannhäuser* and *Lohengrin*, both operas about the Christian 'Knight of Faith'. On page 108, Alexander Fränkel reveals that Bruckner thought seriously about writing an opera with a 'mystical hero like Lohengrin' – so much for the old idea that the composer was unaffected by Wagner's plots. It may also be significant (given the remarks above about the 'impossibility' of Bruckner's infatuations) that both these operas culminate in the hero's renunciation of sexual love.

Some more remarks about sources are necessary. Eckstein, Klose, Hruby and Oberleithner are used extensively because they left whole books of reminiscences, each one of them packed with interesting information which until now has been virtually inaccessible to non-German-speaking readers. Of course I had to be selective. I hestitated over whether to include the chapter 'Mit Anton Bruckner in Mayerling' ('With Anton Bruckner at Mayerling') from Eckstein's *Alte unnennbare Tage!*, but it was difficult to extract sections from this long, elegantly continuous narrative. Perhaps I will repair the omission somewhere else some day. The vast four-volume Göllerich/Auer, *Anton Bruckner. Ein Lebens- und Schaffensbild* could have furnished enough material for a book of reminiscences in itself. And I could happily have gone on collecting rare material from Austrian and German libraries if time had allowed. But I had to draw the line somewhere. My apologies if there are stories I have failed to confirm or deny.

On the whole I have kept to primary, first-hand accounts. Secondary sources have been included when the original is credited and the material is sufficiently interesting. In the end I ruled out Hans Commenda's *Geschichten um Anton Bruckner* ('Stories about Anton Bruckner', Linz, 1946): Commenda does not reveal the origins of any of his anecdotes, and the cover bears the ominous words '*frei den Quellen nacherzählt*' – 'freely retold from the original sources'.

I thought hard about including a story the Norwegian composer Arne Nordheim told me after I had completed the main text, but in the end I decided it would be simpler to record it here. Not long after the end of the Second World War, the young Nordheim hitch-hiked to St Florian, to lay flowers on Bruckner's grave. When Nordheim explained to the sexton what he was doing, the latter invited him to meet two ladies in a nearby old-people's home. These women remembered seeing the tiny figure of Bruckner, in his wide-brimmed hat, with music-paper under his arm, trudging through the snow to the St Florian Chapel, apparently to try out some ideas on the great organ (Nordheim thought this must have been some time in the late 1880s). Amused by Bruckner's appearance, the two girls – as they were then – threw snowballs at him. Far from offended, Bruckner joined in the fight, hurling snow back them with obvious glee. Suddenly he collected himself, waved goodbye and went into the Chapel. The last thing the two women remembered was seeing Bruckner emptying the snow out of his boots before disappearing through the door. Compare that story with other accounts of Bruckner's behaviour with children – by Felix von Kraus (pp. 28–9) and the unnamed member of the Vienna Philharmonic (pp. 80–1) – and it is easy to believe.

Inevitably there were translation problems – especially given my own very limited experience as a translator. Bruckner's dialect caused one the biggest headaches. Some writers reproduce the idiosyncrasies of Bruckner's Upper Austrian speech very vividly. At first I thought about finding an English equivalent. I tried something like Northern English – a dialect I know fairly well – but it looked dreadful on paper. Ultimately I settled for a fairly standard colloquial English. This meant that Carl Hruby's point about how Bruckner's German varied, depending on how excited he was, lost something in translation. The meaning of some of Bruckner's dialect words had to be guessed (none of my Austrian contacts was able to be precise). I thought long and hard about the potentially controversial '*Locherl*' (literally, a 'little hole'), and canvassed opinions from German-speaking friends; my solution, 'arsehole', won by nine votes to one. At the other extreme, I found it impossible to do full justice to Friedrich Klose's accomplished literary style.

As to details, Court and Civil Service ranks have been much simplified; though when their distinctive flavour is essential I have kept to German, as, for instance, when Bruckner calls Gustav Kietz '*Herr Hofrat*' – literally, 'Court Adviser' (p. 138). Place and institution names are given in the English equivalent where possible, unless the result was too cumbersome. I have also harmonized the spelling of names in keeping with their commonest usage.

I would certainly never have attempted to translate so much material without the help and encouragement of friends and colleagues. Katryn Bradshaw, a postgraduate student at Aston University, inspected and corrected some of my efforts and made a few translations of her own when I found I was running out of time. I have edited and restyled her translations and take full responsibility for their final form. The author and translator John Harrison marked some of my earlier attempts and made many helpful suggestions, especially with regard to subordinate clauses (so much more a part of German than of English). In one case, he managed to reduce a twenty-word clause of mine to just five words. In this connection I must also thank Paul Banks, Gunnar Cohrs, Rudiger Görner and Lionel Salter. I am grateful to Brigitte Mauthner and William Meredith Owen for advice on matters psychological. Others provided much-needed help in finding material: Otto Biba, who recommended that I look at Friedrich Eckstein's *Alte unnenbare Tage!* (not listed in any English Bruckner bibliography), John Deathridge, Jonathan Dunsby, Jonathan Del Mar, Elisabeth Maier and Robert Simpson. Thanks too to Andrew Clements, former editor of music books at Faber and Faber, for encouraging me to write this book, and to his successors Michael Durnin and Belinda Matthews for all their efforts. I am deeply grateful to my parents for reading parts of *Bruckner Remembered* and giving their opinions, and especially to my wife Kate, who – though not a 100 per cent Bruckner fan – read though the whole text and made a number of constructive criticisms. It is to her that I dedicate this book.

Stephen Johnson
London, 1996

CHRONOLOGY

BRUCKNER'S LIFE AND WORKS
CONTEMPORARY FIGURES AND EVENTS

1824 [Joseph] Anton Bruckner born, 4 September, at Ansfelden, near Linz, son of Anton Bruckner, a village schoolteacher, and Theresia Bruckner, neé Helm. Anton junior ('Tonerl') is the eldest of the Bruckner children, only five of whom survive infancy

1824 Smetana born.
Beethoven completes Symphony No. 9. Schubert, Quartets in A minor and D minor (*Death and the Maiden*)
Byron dies

1825 Johann Strauss II born. Beethoven, Quartet in A minor, Op. 132

1826 First performance of Weber's *Oberon*. Weber dies
Beethoven, Quartets in C sharp minor, Op. 131, and F major, Op. 135. Schubert completes Symphony in C major (*Great*)

1827 Beethoven dies. Schubert, *Winterreise*

1828 First signs of interest in music, encouraged by both parents. Music lessons with father

1828 Schubert, String Quintet in C, Piano Sonatas in C minor, A major and B flat major, *Schwanengesang*. Schubert dies
Tolstoy born

1829 Rossini completes *William Tell*. Mendelssohn conducts Bach's *St Matthew Passion* in Berlin

1830 Berlioz, *Symphonie fantastique*. Bellini, *I Capuleti ed i Montecchi*. Donizetti, *Anna Bolena*

1831 Pushkin, *Boris Godunov*
Hegel dies

1832 Rossini, *Stabat Mater*
Goethe completes *Faust, Part II*. Goethe dies

1833 Confirmation. B.'s cousin, Johann Baptist Weiss, acts as godfather

1833 Brahms and Borodin born

1834 Begins deputizing for his father as church organist

1834 Berlioz, *Harold in Italy*

1835 Sent to stay with Weiss in nearby Hörsching. Weiss teaches B. harmony and introduces him to choral works by Haydn and Mozart. Probable date of composition of *Pange lingua* for chorus

1835 Donizetti, *Lucia di Lammermoor*

1836 Father's health deteriorates. B. returns to Ansfelden to take over some of his duties

1836 Büchner, *Woyzeck*. Dickens, *The Pickwick Papers*

1837 Bruckner present at the death of his father (7 June). Later that day, his mother takes him to the monastery of St Florian, where he is accepted as a chorister by the prior, Michael Arneth, even though his voice is already breaking. Has lessons in organ, violin and theory. Theresia Bruckner moves to Ebelsberg with B.'s brother Ignaz and sisters Rosalie ('Sali'), Josefa and Maria Anna ('Nani')

1837 Hummel dies. Berlioz, *Grande messe des morts*

1838 Studies organ, piano, violin and figured bass at St Florian

1838 Bizet born

1839 Mussorgsky, Cézanne born

1840 B. decides on a career in teaching. Enters teacher-training college in Linz (1 October). Studies with August Dürrnberger, who introduces B. to the keyboard music of Bach. Hears masses by Mozart, Haydn and Michael Haydn, overtures by Weber and Rossini, and Beethoven's Fourth Symphony

1840 Tchaikovsky born

1841 Passes final exams at teacher-training college. Appointed assistant teacher at Windhaag, near Bohemian border (October). Work is hard, poorly paid and often humiliating

1841 Dvořák, Renoir born

1842 Composes Mass in C. Arneth visits Windhaag and finds B. another teaching post at Krontsdorf, near Steyr

1842 First performance of Wagner's *Rienzi*

1843 B. moves to Krontsdorf, where he is encouraged by his new superior, Franz Lehofer. Studies theory with Leopold von Zenetti in Enns, teaching based on Bach chorales and the *Well-tempered Klavier*. Meets Karoline Eberstaller, a former duet-partner of Schubert, who introduces B. to Schubert's four-hand piano music

1843 Grieg, Henry James born. Hölderlin dies

1844 Composes Mass in F for Maundy Thursday

1844 Rimsky-Korsakov, Nietzsche born

1845 Passes second teaching examination with distinction (29 May). Appointed first assistant teacher at St Florian. Continues studies with Zenetti at Enns

1845 Fauré born

1846 Continues to compose short choral pieces and works for male-voice quartet

1847 Performance of Mendelssohn's *St Paul* in Linz leaves a lasting impression

1847 Mendelssohn dies

1848 Briefly joins National Guard on outbreak of revolution. Appointed provisional organist at St Florian. Brother's godfather Franz Sailer dies, leaving B. his Bösendorfer grand piano. B. begins his first major work, the *Requiem* in D minor, in memory of Sailer

1848 Marx and Engels publish *Communist Manifesto*

February Revolution in France sparks off similar revolutions all over Continental Europe. Metternich resigns, and Franz Joseph I becomes Emperor of Austria and King of Hungary, with Schwarzenberg as prime minister. Risings against Austria in Milan and Venice

1849 First performance of *Requiem* at St Florian (13 March)

1849 Chopin dies. Strindberg born
Mazzini proclaims republic in Rome. Austria defeats Sardinia at Novara and retains control of Northern Italy

1850 Begins two-year course at Linz *Unter-Realschule*. Profoundly disturbed by suicide of cousin and mentor J. B. Weiss. Unsuccessful love-affair with Antonie Werner (16)

1850 Wagner's *Lohengrin* first performed

1851 Works as clerk in local law court. Appointment as organist at St Florian confirmed. First trip to Vienna, to visit composer and court conductor Ignaz Assmayer

1851 First performance of Verdi's *Rigoletto*

1852 Composes *Psalm 114*, *Psalm 22* and *Magnificat* in B flat

1853 Unsuccessful application for post as civil servant. Friends urge B. to devote himself to music

1853 Van Gogh born

1854 Arneth dies. B. composes two works in his memory: *Vor Arneths Grab* and *Libera me*. Composes *Missa solemnis* in B flat minor; first performance at St Florian (14 September)

1854 Britain and France declare war on Russia

1855 Passes *Unter-Realschule* examinations (25–6 January). Organist Robert Führer visits St Florian, sees the *Missa solemnis* and hears B. improvise at the organ. Führer writes B. a glowing testimonial (27 April), and recommends that he study theory with Simon Sechter. B. visits Sechter in Vienna (July) and enroles for a postal course. Wenzel Pranghofer, Linz Cathedral organist, dies, and, after some hesitation, B. auditions successfully for the post (13 November)

1856 Officially appointed organist at Linz Cathedral (25 April). Composes *Ave Maria* for chorus and organ. Begins studies with Sechter, and effectively gives up composition for five years. Finds new mentor and encourager in Franz Josef Rudiger, Bishop of Linz

1856 Schumann, Heine die
Wilde, George Bernard Shaw, Freud born

1857 In addition to duties at the Cathedral and the Parish Church, B. spends up to seven hours each day at his studies for Sechter

1857 Elgar born. Liszt, *Faust* and *Dante* Symphonies
Baudelaire, *Les fleurs du mal.*

1858 Passes examinations in harmony, figured bass and organ playing with distinction (10 July)

1858 Brahms, Piano Concerto No. 1

1859 Passes elementary counterpoint (12 August)

1859 Spohr dies. Wagner completes *Tristan und Isolde.*
First performance of Gounod's *Faust*
Austria defeated by French and Italian forces at Solferino

1860 Passes advanced counterpoint (3 April). Bruckner's mother dies (11 November). Appointed conductor of Linz choral society 'Frohsinn' (November)

1860 Mahler, Wolf, Chekhov born, Schopenhauer dies
Franz Joseph I introduces constitutional reforms

1861 Passes final examination in canon and fugue, thus concluding his studies with Sechter. Composes seven-part *Ave Maria*, performed in Linz, 12 May. Resigns from 'Frohsinn' in response to an ill-judged practical joke. (September). Passes organ examination at Piarists' Church in Vienna (22 November) with outstanding success. *Psalm 146* and *Afferentur regi* first performed at St Florian

(14 December). Begins studies in form and orchestration with Otto Kitzler in Linz

1861 Emancipation of serfs in Russia

1862 B. is introduced to the music of Wagner and Liszt by Kitzler. Work for Kitzler includes String Quartet and four orchestral pieces. Unsuccessful application for organist's post at Imperial Court Chapel

1862 Debussy, Delius, Munch born
Bismarck becomes Prime Minister of Prussia

1863 Hears performance of Wagner's *Tannhäuser* (13 February). Completes Overture in G minor, and composes Symphony in F minor and cantata *Germanenzug*. Passes final examination with Kitzler. Visits Franz Lachner in Munich

1864 Works on a symphony, possibly the D minor (later known as 'No. 0'), but more likely the official Symphony No. 1, in C minor. Completes Mass in D minor (29 September). After the first performance (Linz, 20 November), the critic Moritz von Mayfeld writes that Bruckner's true medium is the symphony. B. takes this as a sign. Amorous disappointments continue. B. informs his friend Rudolf Weinwurm that he is considering emigrating to Russia or Mexico

1864 Richard Strauss born
Marx publishes first volume of *Das Kapital*
Austria forms allegiance with Prussia and defeats Denmark in the war for Schleswig-Holstein

1865 Hears Wagner's *Tristan und Isolde* for the first time in Munich (June). Meets Wagner and von Bülow. Shows beginning of Symphony No. 1 to von Bülow, who encourages him. The critic Eduard Hanslick hears B. improvise and is also warmly encouraging (June). Later meetings with Liszt (Budapest) and Berlioz (Vienna)

1865 Sibelius, Nielsen born

1866 B's sister 'Nani' joins him in Linz. Hears Beethoven's Ninth Symphony for the first time. Completes Symphony No. 1 (14 April) and Mass in E minor (25 November). Falls in love with Josefine Lang (17), and is rejected. Onset of severe depression, followed by nervous breakdown

1866 Busoni, Satie, Kandinsky born
First performance of Smetana's *The Bartered Bride*
Rückert dies. Dostoevsky, *Crime and Punishment* and *The Gambler*
Austria defeated by Prussia in the Seven Weeks War. Bismarck forms North German Confederation, and forces Austria to withdraw from German affairs

1867 At first, B's mental condition shows no sign of improvement. Hints of suicidal thoughts and onset of severe numeromania. Spends three months at the Bad Kreuzen Sanatorium (8 May–8 August) for cold-water cure. Mass in F minor begun at or around this time. Condition improves. Mass in D minor performed in Vienna under Johann Herbeck at Court Chapel. Applications for posts at Vienna University and Court Chapel, both unsuccessful

1867 Wagner completes *Die Meistersinger*
Sholes invents the typewriter
Austria and Hungary form two separate kingdoms under one crown

1868 Re-appointed conductor of choral group 'Frohsinn'. Composes motets *Pange lingua*, *Asperges me* and *Inveni David*. Conducts first performance of finale of Wagner's *Die Meistersinger* (Linz, 4 April). First performance of official Symphony No. 1 (Linz, 9 May). Completes Mass in F minor (9 September). Herbeck visits B. and persuades him to accept Sechter's old post at Vienna Conservatory. Moves to Vienna with sister 'Nani' as housekeeper, and begins teaching (1 October)

1868 Rossini dies
Grieg, Piano Concerto (first version). Brahms completes *A German Requiem*. Stefan Georg born

1869 Visits France, giving organ recitals in Nancy and at Notre Dame, Paris (April–May). Meets French musicians, including Franck and Saint-Saëns. Finishes Symphony in D minor, later known as 'No. 0' (12 September). First performance of Mass in E minor in new Linz Cathedral (25 September). Vienna Philharmonic rejects Symphony No. 1

1869 Pfitzner, Gide, Matisse born. Berlioz dies
Tolstoy completes *War and Peace*

1870 Death of 'Nani' (16 January). Katharina Kachelmayr ('Frau Kathi') becomes B's new housekeeper. B. takes up teaching post at St Anna teacher-training college

1870 Dickens dies. Lenin born
Outbreak of Franco-Prussian War

1871 Visits London to give organ recitals at Albert Hall and Crystal Palace (August). Back in Vienna B. faces disciplinary action over remarks made to one of his girl pupils. Begins Symphony No. 2 (October) and makes sketches for a symphony in B flat

1871 Proust born
End of Franco-Prussian War. France loses Alsace-Lorraine. German Reich formed, with Wilhelm I (formally King of Prussia) as Emperor and Bismarck as Chancellor

1872 Conducts first performance of Mass in F minor at Augustinian Church, Vienna (16 June). The work is warmly praised by Brahms, Hanslick and Liszt. Completes Symphony No. 2 (11 September), which is rejected as 'unplayable' by Vienna Philharmonic. First ideas for Symphony No. 3 (October)

1872 Vaughan Williams and Skryabin born
George Eliot, *Middlemarch*
Formation of the *Dreikaiserbund* between Emperors of Germany, Austria and Russia

1873 Continues work on Symphony No. 3 (completed, 31 December). Visits spas at Marienbad and Karlsbad, continuing to Bayreuth (September) to meet Wagner, who accepts the dedication of Symphony No. 3. Conducts first performance of Symphony No. 2 in Vienna (26 October)

1873 Rakhmaninov born

1874 Composes Symphony No. 4, 'Romantic' (completed 22 November). Death of sister Josefa at St Florian (13 July). Application for post at Vienna University opposed by Hanslick. Loses post at St Anna College, with dire financial consequences. Symphony No. 3 is partially revised, and rejected by the Vienna Philharmonic

1874 Schoenberg, Ives born

1875 Begins Symphony No. 5 (February), and makes sketches for another *Requiem* in D minor. Appointed lecturer in harmony and counterpoint at Vienna University, but only in an 'honorary' (i.e. unpaid) capacity

1875 Bizet dies. Ravel, Rilke, Thomas Mann, Jung born

1876 Completes first draft of Symphony No. 5 (16 May) and immediately begins work on revision. Symphony No. 2 performed again in Vienna (February) to a mixed reception. Attends first complete performance of Wagner's *Ring* cycle at Bayreuth in summer. Revises the three numbered masses and Symphony No. 3 (including new version of Adagio)

1876 Brahms completes Symphony No. 1
First telephonic transmission of human voice by Alexander Graham Bell in USA

1877 Moves to new appartment. Position at University confirmed, with salary. Symphony No. 3 accepted by Vienna Philharmonic. First performance, conducted by B. (16 December), is disastrous. Nevertheless Theodor Rättig offers to publish the work in orchestral score and four-hand piano arrangement (by Mahler and Rudolf Krzyzanowski)

1877 Tolstoy completes *Anna Karenina*

1878 Complete revision of Symphony No. 4, and partial revision of Nos. 3 and 5. Composes motet *Tota pulchra es* and *Abendzauber*. Begins String Quintet on suggestion of Josef Hellmesberger, director of the Conservatory and leader of a famous quartet

1878 Brahms, Symphony No. 2. Tchaikovsky's Symphony No. 4 first performed

1879 Completes String Quintet (12 July) and composes motet *Os justi*. Begins Symphony No. 6. Hellmesberger rejects the Scherzo of the String Quintet as 'too difficult'; B. composes a substitute movement, Intermezzo in D minor (December)

1879 Ibsen, *A Doll's House*
Einstein born

1880 Revision of Symphony No. 4 completed. Visits Oberammergau and tours Switzerland. First signs of persistent leg and foot troubles

1880 Robert Musil born. George Eliot dies. Dostoevsky, *The Brothers Karamazov*

1881 Symphony No. 4 first performed in Vienna under Hans Richter (20 February), with great success. Begins *Te Deum* and completes Symphony No. 6 (3 September). Three weeks later, B. begins work on Symphony No. 7. First performance of String Quintet (without finale), 17 November

1881 Bartók, Stefan Zweig, Picasso born. Musorgsky, Dostoevsky die
Ibsen, *Ghosts*. Henry James, *Portrait of a Lady*
Assassination of Tsar Alexander II

1882 Visit to Bayreuth for first performance of *Parsifal*. B. sees Wagner for the last time

1882 Stravinsky, Joyce, Virginia Woolf born
Formation of Triple Alliance between Germany, Italy and Austria-Hungary

1883 Premonition of Wagner's death inspires B. to begin Adagio of Symphony No. 7 (January). First performance of 2nd and 3rd movements of Symphony No. 6 (11 February). B. visits Wagner's grave at Bayreuth. Symphony No. 7 completed (7 September). Second version of *Te Deum* begun (28 September)

1883 Webern, Kafka born. Wagner, Karl Marx die
Brahms, Symphony No. 3

1884 *Te Deum* completed (7 March). First complete performance of String Quintet (May). B. goes to Leipzig for triumphant première of Symphony No. 7 under Arthur Nikisch (7 December). Also visits Prague and Munich. Final setting of liturgical text *Christus factus est*. Begins work on Symphony No. 8

1884 Smetana dies

1885 Composes motets *Virga Jesse* and *Ecce sacerdos*. Munich première of Symphony No. 7 under Hermann Levi (10 March), great success. Symphony No. 3 performed in New York

1885 Berg, Varèse, D. H. Lawrence born
Brahms completes Symphony No. 4
Nietzsche completes *Also sprach Zarathustra*. Wilde, *The Importance of Being Earnest*

1886 First performance of *Te Deum* (Vienna, 10 January), and Vienna première of Symphony No. 7 (21 March). Receives the Order of Franz Josef (9 July) and is received by the Emperor (23 September). Visits Bayreuth to hear *Tristan* and play the organ at Liszt's funeral (3 August)

1886 Liszt dies

1887 Appointed honorary member of Maatschappij tot Bevordering der Toonkunst, Amsterdam. London première of Symphony No. 7 (23 May), not well received. Symphony No. 8 completed and dispatched to Levi (4 September). Symphony No. 9 begun (21 September). Levi's rejection of Symphony No. 8 causes severe depression and nervous irritability. B. begins extensive revision of Symphonies Nos. 8 and 4

1887 Borodin dies
First performance of Verdi's *Otello*
Strindberg, *The Father*

1888 Successes in Vienna and Prague fail to console B. Begins revision of Symphony No. 3 with Franz Schalk

1888 T. S. Eliot born
Wilhem I of Germany dies. Succeeded briefly by Frederick III, then by Wilhelm II

1889 Created honorary member of Richard Wagner Society. Revision of Symphony No. 3 completed (11 February). Work on Symphony No. 8 continues

1889 Wittgenstein born
Death of Crown Prince Rudolf of Austria at Mayerling

1890 Health gradually deteriorates. Created honorary member of the Austrian Diet, with stipendiary salary. Gives up professorship (organ) at Conservatory. Revision of Symphony No. 8 completed (10 March). Begins revision of Symphony No. 1. Plays for the wedding of the Emperor's daughter, Princess Marie Valerie, at Ischl (31 July)

1890 Franck, Van Gogh die
Wilhelm I of Germany forces Bismarck to resign

1891 Completes revision of Symphony No. 1 (18 April). Visits Berlin for performance of *Te Deum*, where he proposes to a young chambermaid, Ida Buhz, and is apparently accepted (though the marriage never takes place). Receives Honorary Doctorate from Vienna University (7 November), and resumes work on Symphony No. 9

1891 Prokofiev born. Brahms completes Clarinet Trio and Clarinet Quintet

1892 Resigns from Court Chapel. Composes *Psalm 150*, *Das deutsche Lied*, and *Vexilla regis*. First performance of Symphony No. 8 under Richter (18 December)

1892 Maeterlinck's *Pelléas et Mélisande* published

1893 Created honorary member of Gesellschaft der Musikfreunde. Completes *Helgoland* for male chorus and orchestra (7 August). Health deteriorates further. B. makes his will. Work on Symphony No. 9 continues sporadically

1893 Tchaikovsky, Gounod die
First performance of Tchaikovsky's Symphony No. 6
Munch, *The Scream*

1894 B.'s condition improves. Travels to Berlin with Hugo Wolf to hear performances of his own works (January), but suffers a setback soon afterwards, and is unable to attend first performance of Symphony No. 5 in Graz (8 April). Celebrates 70th birthday in Steyr, and receives many honours. Resigns from University. Adagio of Symphony No. 9 completed. Begins work on finale

1894 First performance of Debussy's *Prélude à l'après-midi d'un faune*

1895 Struggles to continue work on finale of Symphony No. 9, despite deteriorating physical and mental health. Moves to gatekeeper's lodge at Schloss Belvedere on invitation of Emperor (July)

1895 Hindemith born.
First performances of Strauss's *Till Eulenspiegel* and Mahler's Symphony No. 2 (*Resurrection*)

1896 Attends performance of his own music for the last time (12 January): concert includes *Te Deum* and Richard Strauss's *Till Eulenspiegel*. Health declines still further, though finale of Symphony No. 9 possibly completed in sketch score. B. dies, 11 October. Funeral at the Kalskirche, Vienna, 14 October. B.'s body subsequently interred in the crypt at St Florian, below the great organ

1896 First performance of Puccini's *La bohème*

I

VOCATION

Joseph Anton Bruckner was born on 4 September 1824, in the Upper Austrian village of Ansfelden, about ten miles south of Linz. He was the eldest of five surviving children born to Anton Bruckner (1791–1837), schoolteacher and organist, and his wife Theresia, *née* Helm (1801–60), a keen singer, evidently with a good voice. The young Anton ('Tonerl') soon showed signs of musical talent, which his parents encouraged. At four, he was playing hymns on a miniature violin, progressing quickly to the family spinet; and by the age of ten he was able to stand in for his father as church organist. By then he had also made his first visit to the Augustian monastery of St Florian, a few miles to the east of Ansfelden, which in later years was to become his spiritual home. With the arrival of three younger sisters, Rosalie ('Sali'), Josefa and Maria Anna ('Nani'), and brother Ignaz, the house was now too full, so in 1835 the young Anton was sent to nearby Hörsching to stay with his godfather and cousin Johann Baptist Weiss (1813–50), a respected local composer and organist who taught Bruckner music theory (including figured bass) and introduced him to choral works by Mozart and Haydn. The following year, Anton senior became seriously ill; he died, of consumption, in 1837. Soon afterwards Bruckner entered St Florian as a chorister.

IGNAZ BRUCKNER

As the style of this reminiscence shows, the composer's only surviving brother, Ignaz, was what used to be called a 'simple soul' (his spelling defies translation). From 1851, Ignaz was a gardener at St Florian, until his eyesight began to deteriorate, after which he worked as a servant in the monastery, one of his duties being the operation of the bellows for the great organ. He remained close to his brother and in 1893 he was named, along with his sister Rosalie, as the composer's heir. He died in 1913.

I don't know anything about our father when he was well. But I remember him when he was sick, how he once called me by name – I ran away. I can remember him lying in bed . . .

Mother said father was just like my brother. In later years, brother got more robust.

When father died, he was wearing a black cassock and a black nightcap.

I liked the music (at the funeral). I laughed then. The woman gravedigger said to me. 'You musn't laugh, it's your father that's died.'

I still know what the food was at the funeral. It was on a day of fasting so we had *Grießschmarrn* [semolina pancakes]. Otherwise we'd've had beef with bread dumplings and horseradish and rice with raisins too!

The last thing I can remember is how we got to Ebelsberg.

I don't know anything about my brother – he never played with me – he had bigger friends than me.

He often told us how he played robbers in the meadows with the other boys. They always caught him and then whacked him with sticks on his backside. But he put heavily patched trousers on so he couldn't feel anything. That really pleased him, when they hit him so hard and he felt nothing.

Father noticed when he came home late because of the singing lessons. When he caught him by the hair he just got a lump of it – brother slipped away and father did nothing to him . . .

Brother's patrons always died too soon. He was more demanding than anyone else can ever have been. In the last years he said, 'Some day you've got to hear one of my symphonies!' I said, 'I don't understand anything about them.' 'It doesn't matter,' he shouted, 'you've still got to listen to one!'

Our sister Anna was in Linz and Vienna as brother's housekeeper. She was our favourite. Mother still prayed for her on her deathbed. She said that he (Anton) should look after her instead of mother, since she was so weak.

She was the eleventh and the last.*

Brother looked after her. Unfortunately she died early, in 1870. She's got her own grave in the cemetery in Währing.

[Göllerich/Auer, I, 67–72]

KARL SEIBERL

The son of a headmaster from St Marienkirchen, Karl Seiberl went to the Monastery of St Florian as a chorister in 1839, two years after Bruckner. He went on to study law, eventually becoming a councillor in the Higher Regional Court (*Oberlandesgerichtsrat*) at Wels. He was to remain on friendly terms with Bruckner until the composer's death, though according to Seiberl their musical differences became more marked in the 1870s: 'Bruckner was Wagnerian, whilst I remained true to Mozart.' Seiberl's account is written in a very plain, matter-of-fact style which doesn't always make for easy reading (one enormous, largely redundant parenthesis in paragraph four has been removed), but it is full of useful information. His final remark is striking: despite the evidence of his exceptional talent, Bruckner was evidently far from convinced about his musical vocation.

In 1839 I became a chorister in the monastery of St Florian. There I got to know Anton Bruckner, the son of a schoolmaster from Ansfelden. Bruckner was also a chorister; but he was fifteen years old and his voice had already broken, so he was now used as a violinist rather than as a singer. He was given his first basic training in organ continuo playing by his cousin, Johann Weiss, schoolmaster at Hörsching – he was also Bruckner's sponsor – and it was Weiss who brought him to St Florian as a chorister in 1837. Schoolmaster Weiss was an excellent organist, much valued by Schiedermayr, at that time cathedral organist in Linz; Schiedermayr always let Weiss play the organ whenever he appeared in the choir of the old Linz cathedral – a special honour. I know this from my

*Most sources state that Theresia Bruckner gave birth to eleven children, but according to Manfred Wagner the baptismal records at Ansfelden name twelve. [Wagner: *Bruckner – Leben, Werke, Dokumente*, p. 23]

brother, Josef Seiberl, who died in 1908 while he was headmaster in St Marienkirchen an der Polsenz. Between 1843 and 1847 he was assistant teacher at Hörsching, and often witnessed the conversations between Weiss and Bruckner, whom my brother had befriended on the teacher-training course, whenever the latter came to visit his cousin in Hörsching.

According to my brother's description, Johann Weiss was a very talented musician with an excellent memory, which meant that he could play Haydn's *Seasons* and *Creation* off by heart. He was a magnificent improviser at the organ, as he showed to advantage in the chapel at St Florian, where he gave concerts with the monastery organist Kattinger and with Bruckner. The three organists – Kattinger (a Master organist for whom Bruckner had the highest respect) at the great organ. Bruckner and Weiss on the two side-organs – improvised on a theme given by Kattinger. I myself was not present at this coming together of the three finest organists in the region and beyond, and therefore missed what must have been a great musical event. But my brother Josef was there, and he told me that for most of those acutely attentive listeners, it was schoolmaster Weiss who made the most positive impression. From this, Weiss gave Bruckner a firm foundation in organ playing, on which he would be able to build later. And that is exactly what Bruckner did. Through his great talent and his tireless dedication to his theoretical studies, by listening to the outstanding monastery organist Kattinger and to the classical church and chamber music nurtured at the Stift, and with the firm foundation of Weiss's teaching, Bruckner was able to progress from year to year without rest until he grew into the figure that we admired so much.

As mentioned above, Bruckner often visited my brother when he was Weiss's assistant at Hörsching. On one such visit, when Bruckner again showed his unquestionable ability, Weiss said to my brother, 'Watch him, one day he'll make a name for himself.' Weiss did not live to see the fulfilment of his prophecy; he died too soon. A pity – perhaps Weiss could also have made a name for himself if his talent had found the right channels.

During the teacher-training course (in Linz) Bruckner lived, with perhaps a landlady, in a little one-storey house in the Bethlehemstrasse [. . .] where I visited him. After the completion of the course

I did not see Bruckner again until 1846, when he was assistant teacher at Kronstorf. Bruckner played to me on the organ, ending, as usual, with a fugue, whose theme he took from the folk-hymn with which he had begun. He also took me to the nearby farmhouse where he was always met with a warm reception and had the opportunity to play on a piano that belonged to the farmer. Between 1845 and 1855 Bruckner was a teacher at St Florian. At that time I was at the grammar school in Linz, and I walked over to the monastery as often as I could. Thanks to the benevolence of the Prelate Arneth and the other canons, especially the *Regens chori* (choir-leader) Traumihler, St Florian became my second home, in which I could easily feel like a member of the brotherhood.

Naturally I often met Bruckner there, and I know that it was during this time that he came to possess his valuable 'Bösendorfer'. If my memory serves me right, it was part of an exhibition held in a country house in Linz in 1848.* It was bought by Sailer, the court scribe who was employed by the monastery, and given to Bruckner as a present. This instrument, which served Bruckner to the very end, is now preserved at the monastery of St Florian.

Bruckner became organist at St Florian at the beginning of 1849, as the previous organist Kattinger went to Kremsmünster as a tax official after the Revolution of 1848. In March 1855 I too came to St Florian, after completing my university studies. As a legal practitioner, I made my probation with the regional authority, of which Schiedermayr, the son of the Linz Cathedral organist, was in charge. I had not been to St Florian since 1850, and so I was delighted to able to go there again and see my friend Bruckner. Strange! Bruckner's behaviour was friendly enough, but he did not seem especially pleased to see me. Instead he was morose and taciturn, and I wondered what the problem was. One day Bruckner asked me, 'Seiberl, do you think that if I had studied I would also have been a lawyer, or would I have become a priest?' A priest, I replied, since he was such a devout person. Bruckner did not seem at all pleased with this answer. Before long he began studying for

*In 1847 there was a commercial exhibition in the ballrooms of several local country houses [Seiberl's note]. In fact, Sailer bequeathed the piano to Bruckner at his death in 1848 [SJ].

the grammar school, taking lessons from a canon whose name I cannot mention, throwing himself with typical dedication into learning Latin. It turned out that he had already studied the other subjects on the teacher-training and lower state secondary school courses so that he would know enough to enter the grammar school. He meant to become a lawyer and then a civil servant.

[Gräflinger, 100–103]

MAX VON OBERLEITHNER

The composer Max von Oberleithner (1868–1935) was the son of a wealthy industrialist in Mähren. He graduated in music from the Vienna University, then in 1890 he became a private student of Bruckner on the recommendation of the conductor and composer Felix Mottl. They became close, and in 1892 Bruckner dedicated his last great choral work, *Psalm 150*, to his pupil. Oberleithner's book *Meine Erinnerungen an Anton Bruckner* ('My memories of Anton Bruckner') is a particularly rich source of information about the composer. The following passage occurs in a chapter with the self-explanatory title 'Episodes from Bruckner's life, as he himself told them'; it is not therefore a primary recollection of the younger Bruckner, rather a memory of a recollection. The material it contains is, however, sufficiently interesting to justify its inclusion here.

Anton Bruckner was thirteen years old when his father died. When one of the priests at the Monastery of St Florian asked him what he would like to be, he replied, 'What my father was.'

As a result he was trained as a teacher at the monastery's expense. At that time this was a hard career, wretchedly paid, and perpetually subordinate to the clergy. His first post was as 'assistant teacher' in Windhaag, and later he moved to Kronstorf, and a salary of twenty florins a year.

It was while he was in Kronstorf that he fell in love with the sister of the parish priest. This was the only time a woman returned his feelings, for his later inamoratas were all 'Salsen', ('trollops' – Bruckner's own description). She still wrote to him when he found a better position at St Florian, asking if it was all over between them. She got married later, when Bruckner was cathedral organist in Linz, and died shortly after giving birth.

In spite of all trials and tribulations, Bruckner managed to obtain a post as organist at St Florian, though his musical education was no more than was normal for a trainee teacher, and as an organist he was actually self-taught. His first musical impressions – hearing Schubert *Lieder* at the monastery, and the playing of the organist Kattinger – fired his enthusiasm so strongly that he was able, through unparalleled diligence, to make the transition from teacher to musician.

As a musician, Bruckner made sure he always honoured St Cecilia's Day. Especially in 1852 – 'I made a colossal idiot of myself then.' The drink was punch, and in proposing a toast to the saint, Bruckner held forth on her life and works without knowing much about either. But on the way home he lost the key to the great organ, and he was to play the next morning at seven o'clock. How could he find it again? There was nothing for it but to get the boys up early and set them looking; fortunately they found the missing key with time to spare.

Bruckner seems to have spent rather more time in lively company in those early days. As he himself told me, 'The Prelate Arneth used to like me a lot, but he changed his tune.' He once said that if the visits to the tavern didn't stop soon, he would have Bruckner and the organ thrown out. 'It struck me that if the Herr Prelate had thrown both me and the organ out together, things would have been all right. I wrote a cantata for the Herr Prelate's name-day and he arranged for me to get thirty florins holiday money in return. But I wasn't able to thank him; he never let me.'

[Oberleithner, 72–4]

MATTHIAS LEUTGÄB

At the time he wrote this reminiscence, Matthias Leutgäb was a headmaster in the town of Enns, about five miles east of St Florian. He was a friend of Leopold von Zenetti, who taught Bruckner from 1843 to 1846 and encouraged him to compose: the results included a

> Mass in F for Maundy Thursday and several shorter liturgical works. Leutgäb was present at Bruckner's audition for the position of organist at Linz cathedral in November 1855. Bruckner applied for this post when it fell vacant after the death of the previous organist, Wenzel Pranghofer. To those who knew him, Bruckner would have been the obvious successor to Pranghofer; but it seems he had to be virtually bullied into going to Linz on the day of the audition and, on arriving, he needed further gentle coercion from his teacher, August Dürrnberger, to take part in the examination. Once he did, though, the outcome was obvious.

Some time has elapsed since I was in contact with Bruckner. At the beginning of the fifties, he was an assistant teacher at Kronstorf. He undertook a course in harmony, and his work was judged 'good', but he studied very diligently and in time achieved complete mastery. His first instrument was a so-called spinet: a rectangular box, finely strung, that could be set down on a table. In later years he wanted to buy the spinet back, but it had vanished without trace, for when Bruckner moved on, the spinet ended up in the loft. There it was exposed to the elements, fell apart, and the schoolmaster's children took the strings one by one when they needed some wire.

Herr von Zenetti, a fine organist and composer, played an important part in Bruckner's education. He supported Bruckner by giving him proper work, excellent church music and practical advice. Later, when Bruckner was appointed Court Organist, he remembered Zenetti with gratitude. Whenever he stayed at St Florian he would pay a visit to Enns and spend a few convivial hours with his old teacher. It was during these visits that I got to know him better. After the death of the Linz organist Pranghofer he held the post provisionally – I was then still at my studies. When the auditions for the post were held there were five [*sic*] candidates. They were heard one afternoon in the old cathedral. The only people present were the members of the committee and the applicants. Each player was given a fugue theme, on which he had to improvise. One of them was handed a theme in the minor key, but he handed it back because it was beyond him. Bruckner listened eagerly. He was the last to play. Before he did so, Professor Dürrnberger called softly to us in the church, 'Listen to this, now we'll hear the real thing.'

Bruckner performed his task with highest mastery, especially in his varied use of the organ stops, and with this his appointment was assured. His achievements in Linz are well known. I should only add that during a conference of local teachers he delighted us in church with his playing. Later on, I was a regular guest at St Florian on holy days and attended his organ recitals; in later years these became more obscure because of his growing absorption in the music of Wagner. He was a diligent worker and a hearty eater. His appetite was well catered for by the monks. His favourite dish was strudel, and for his sake it often appeared on the table. At St Florian, everyone went to their rooms after the evening meal; but Bruckner would go and spend a few hours at the Gasthaus, drinking rough cider with his old friends.

[Gräflinger, 91–2]

BRUCKNER'S AUDITION AT LINZ

The record of Bruckner's audition for the post of organist at Linz cathedral survives. It confirms accounts that Bruckner was the outstanding candidate, by some margin. The concluding testimonial to Bruckner's character and 'scholarly' accomplishment should also be noted.

Record

Written in the Sacristy of the Cathedral of Linz, 25 January 1856, in the presence of the undersigned committee-members.

Object

The examination, in sequence, of candidates for the vacant post of Cathedral and Parish Organist in Linz.

Registered Candidates

1. Georg Müller, private music-teacher from Linz,
2. Ludwig Paupie, organist of the Parish Church in Wels,
3. Raimund Hain, assistant teacher at the Parish School of St Mathias in Linz and organist of the same,

4. Anton Bruckner, formerly organist at St Florian and currently provisional cathedral and parish organist at Linz.

This examination was carried out at the cathedral organ, in the above-written order, to themes prepared by the undersigned K. &. K. Ordinarius Professor of Continuo and Choral Singing, with the following results.

I. Georg Müller played through the easy B major theme given to him quite simply, without any contrapuntal elaboration, passing instead into the mechanical execution of a prelude, which lacked structure and coherence and showed, in its mundane way, a complete lack of proper education in counterpoint and technique. The candidate left secretly soon afterwards, of his own volition, and did not sit the further examination in choral accompaniment.

II. Ludwig Paupie was given a theme in C minor which was considered appropriate to one of his position and experience, but he handed it back, declaring that it was too difficult, and asked for an easier theme. With the approval of all present, he was given the one in D major. Instead of developing this theme artfully however, he lapsed quickly into the execution of a prelude, in which he nevertheless showed a certain mechanical competence; of the higher plane of strict contrapuntal style however, and of the artistic riches that spring from it, he showed no knowledge. He performed the desired choral accompaniment as though this were quite alien to him, and as a result, his attempt was unsatisfactory.

III. Raimund Hain, following the wishes of everyone present, took the theme in D major that had defeated his predecessor. He elaborated it contrapuntally, in combination with a second theme, very worthily, if not quite in the strictest style. His choral accompaniment was equally satisfactory, and in this he showed the level of artistry required of a respectable organist in the position concerned; however for some considerable time he has shown a noticeable inability to go beyond this level, and signs of a determined, intelligent striving after the highest perfection and complete mastery are lacking.

IV. Anton Bruckner was invited to take the theme in C minor that Paupie had rejected as too difficult. He declared himself willing, and developed it in a rigorous, skilful, formally complete fugue. He then performed the choral accompaniment with outstanding accomplishment and perfection to the delight of all present, showing that very excellence which is already apparent in his command of the organ, and not least in his well-known and soundly composed liturgical works.

The outcome of these individual performances was the unanimous decision that out of all the above-named candidates, Anton Bruckner should with justice be preferred; not only so, but taking into consideration the important and influential position of a cathedral organist as regards the reputation of the first and foremost church in the diocese, his role as model and lofty example of religious artistry to all other organists in the diocese, and the necessity arising from his position that there should be general recognition and respect for his personal authority in the highest technical and scholarly matters, especially in the obligatory educational work, or in the case of any doubts arising about his true commitment to his post, only Anton Bruckner, on account of his long, dedicated and enthusiastic studies and his tireless technical training, could be counted fully worthy and equal to this calling.

With which this record is concluded and confirmed by the authority of the assembled committee-members at the date given above.

For the Reverend Domscholaster
and Parish-Administrator
J. Storch mp.
Senior.
Franz Gugeneder mp.
Sacristry-Director and Ordinariat Cv.
A. M. Storch
Vinzenz Fink,
Deputy Congregational Representative
J. Aug. Dürrnberger,
K. &. K. Ordinarius Professor of Continuo and Choral Singing
Georg Arminger,
Cathedral Vicar and Vicar-Choral

[Gräflinger, 21–3]

KARL SEIBERL

Bruckner's triumph at the Linz audition should have put an end to his doubts about his future career, but the next extract from Karl Seiberl's recollection shows him still thinking of entering the legal profession. That Bruckner could have found time to study Latin and Law seriously is astonishing: his duties at the cathedral and at the parish church, his private piano tuition and rigorous daily practice regime demanded an enormous amount of time and energy. Even after Bruckner decided to devote himself to musical studies with the eminent theorist Simon Sechter, his obsessive thoroughness could be alarming. 'I implore you to take more care of yourself and to allow yourself sufficient relaxation,' Sechter wrote to Bruckner; 'I must tell you that I have never had a more dedicated pupil.'

In 1855 I finished my legal probation at St Florian. I got a position in the Linz District Court. In the same year Bruckner came to Linz to take up the post of cathedral organist after the death of Pranghofer – the same Pranghofer that wrote the motto of the Linz male-voice choir 'Frohsinn'. A number of people formed a group around the candidates, amongst them the teacher Engelbert Lanz of Linz. All the applicants had to undergo an examination at the organ. Bruckner's playing was so masterly that Lanz, deeply impressed, said to him, 'Bruckner, you'll be the death of us!'

Bruckner became cathedral organist in Linz. At that time we ran into each other only by chance. All I know about him is that he was continuing his Latin studies with a student in the upper part of the grammar school, and that his social life centred on the guest-house 'Zum Bayrischen Hof' (now 'Zaininger'), where he had his lunch, and where he was able to meet lawyers, whose company he preferred.

In the autumn of 1856 I came to Weyr as an actuary. Before I left, I met Bruckner in the Kollegiengasse, and on finding out that he was still working away at his law studies, I encouraged him – almost begged him – to knock all that useless stuff out of his head. His great talent showed him the way. He should go to Vienna and continue to study music theory with Sechter,* and thus become a great man! I do not know whether my advice had any influence on him; all I can report is that from 1857 onwards, Bruckner did indeed continue his studies with Sechter.

[Gräflinger, 103–4]

Bruckner's musical studies, with Sechter, then with the German conductor Otto Kitzler (form and orchestration), lasted until July 1863, when the composer was nearly thirty-nine. It was only then, Bruckner recalled, that he at last felt like 'a watchdog who'd broken his chain'. Three weeks after his fortieth birthday, Bruckner completed his Mass in D minor, the work most commentators acknowledge as his first fully mature large-scale composition. (It was this work which caused Moritz von Mayfeld to make the prophetic remark quoted below.) However, two further formative experiences – the first encounters with Wagner's *Tristan und Isolde* (1865) and Beethoven's Ninth Symphony (1866) – were still to come.

MAX VON OBERLEITHNER

Bruckner told of a certain Herr Mayfeld, a political official he had known in his Linz days who also happened to be a very good pianist. After the performance of the First Mass, Mayfeld wrote in a Linz newspaper that the symphony was Bruckner's true medium. 'I felt this was a pointer in the right direction.'

At this time there was a Kapellmeister Dorn at the Linz Stadttheater, who encouraged Bruckner in modernist, Wagnerian directions. Dorn was able to play the First Symphony from the score. While he was still young, he went mad and died shortly afterwards. Dorn must have made an impression on Bruckner, because in later years he appeared in one of the composer's dreams, as he told me: 'You know, Dorn appeared to me in a dream and said, "The first three movements of the Romantic (Fourth) Symphony are ready, and we'll soon find the theme for the fourth.

*Bruckner had in fact visited Sechter in July 1855 and arranged a postal course in strict harmony and counterpoint.

Go to the piano and play it for me." I was so excited I woke up, leaped out of bed and wrote the theme down, just as I'd heard it from him.' However, this was not to be the final version of the finale. Later Bruckner discarded that dream-inspired theme.

[Oberleithner, 74–5]

Bruckner did indeed rewrite the finale of his Fourth Symphony, twice; but the main theme, first presented in a massive, full-orchestral unison in E flat minor, remains in the same form (except for a few tiny details of scoring) in the recompositions of 1878 and 1880. Was this – despite Oberleithner's final claim – the 'dream-inspired' theme? If so, its retention in the revisions could well be a mark of Bruckner's respect for Ignaz Dorn.

FERDINAND KRACKOWIZER

Dr Ferdinand Krackowizer, Linz district archivist, writer and music-lover, evidently sang under Bruckner's direction on several occasions, and he appears to have been a member of the glee club 'Frohsinn' (literally 'gaiety') which Bruckner conducted in 1860–61 and 1868–9. He presents a portrait of Bruckner in his early forties, at the height of his reputation in Linz. Krackowizer refers to two works: *Germanenzug*, for male chorus and brass, was first performed in June 1865; the 'extremely difficult vocal mass' is the E minor Mass, for chorus and wind, premièred at the consecration of the votive chapel of the new Linz cathedral (29 September 1869).

Bruckner, who at that time was an imposing forty-year-old, was an extremely fit man. His intelligent, round head covered with short-cropped brown hair sat on top of his strong, well-nourished body. His friendly, tanned face smiled warmly at everyone. His bright eyes looked out onto the world with sincere contentment. His black cloth suit, which was wide, comfortable and full of creases, must have been made by a somewhat mediocre tailor. Round his slim neck was a very wide shirt collar, around which a black silk scarf had been loosely thrown. A fine roman nose gave his face a dignified expression. He was clean-shaven and wore only an insignificant little pencil moustache, closely trimmed in the English fashion. His biographers are not wrong in comparing his head to that of an emperor, provided they are describing the *old* man. However, at that time in his life, dear, kind Bruckner bore no resemblance to Caesar. He was the finest example of a genuine, respectable, cheerful Upper Austrian. Nevertheless, despite his unassuming appearance, he was noticed wherever he went. The whole of the town knew this charming man, and everybody enjoyed watching him as he hurried through the streets towards the river Danube on which Linz stood. He would chatter away to his snuff box, an extraordinarily large blue handkerchief stuffed in his jacket pocket. In the evening, amongst friends, he liked to smoke a Cuban cigar and loved a glass of good wine – or maybe several. He had a splendid appetite, though I will mention this only briefly, because some of his biographers have mentioned everything he ate in great detail. The fact that the strong, healthy man, who began his duties in the church choir very early in the morning, then had to give exhausting piano lessons to private pupils and on many evenings hold choir rehearsals, needed a more substantial amount of food than the pale-faced office workers and teachers is natural. When he dashed into the 'Bayerischen Hof' inn on a Friday, he didn't see the friendly greetings of his loyal admirers to his left and right, but went straight up to the waiter and asked him anxiously: 'Josef, have you any crab soup?' If the assiduous young servant answered in the affirmative then Bruckner would shout to him: 'Josef, bring me three portions quickly!' He always ordered triple servings of his favourite dishes – lamb 'Beuschel', offal with dumplings or mutton with turnips. Sometimes, after the meal, the organ Master and I would look out of the window onto the street. Once we saw some fair young maids, smiling and looking conspicuously over at us from the pub opposite. Bruckner was very curious to know who the 'ladies' were, and he was shocked to discover that they were girls of a very obliging character, the kind we in Linz called 'Flitscherln'.* Outraged, he stepped back from the window.

*A delightfully expressive Austrian dialect word, from the German *Flittchen*: 'floosies' would be the nearest English equivalent.

Looking out from the terrace of the then-thriving inn 'Zum Roten Krebs' (The Red Crab), there was a lovely view of the powerful Danube and the rolling hills of the Mühlviertel. It was for this reason that, when the weather was nice, the terrace was full of customers, laughing and enjoying a meal. On 5 May 1868, I sat cheerfully amongst them, having lunch with a jolly, friendly old man from Steyr, who was an exceptional *basso profundo* in a choral society and the guardian of two charming young ladies. Bruckner, a good friend of the amiable bass-singer, had sat down with us and was busy chatting enthusiastically to the beautiful Johanna. Master Anton derived particular pleasure from talking to nice women, as well as musicians, and it cannot be denied that he was particularly susceptible to Cupid's arrows. Suddenly all the customers noticed a large group of people shouting and rushing towards the bridge. The stability of the wooden bridge span, which was constantly battered by the waves of the surging Danube, had been threatened by the impact of iron tugboats which a steamship was supposedly towing upstream. Suddenly, some of the pillars of the bridge collapsed like playing cards, unfortunately throwing some people into the water with them. Deeply shocked by this horrific sight, Johanna sank into the arms of Master Bruckner, who was standing next to her, and who comforted her lovingly. Long after this event, the infatuated forty-year-old continued to court the young girl from Steyr ardently. He would often ask me: 'Do you think Johanna likes me?' But the object of Bruckner's admiration never remained the same for any great length of time.

The position of choirmaster of the glee club 'Frohsinn' caused Bruckner a lot of bother. The rehearsals were held in Bethlehemstrasse in a room of the 'Nordico', a former education establishment for Catholic boys from Sweden and Norway. He detested working at the choral sweetmeats of Franz Abt or lively Viennese waltzes, but he did it, as he did everything, thoroughly and conscientiously. However, it was with great enthusiasm that he rehearsed his own beautiful choral composition *Germanenzug*.

Later, rehearsals took place in a newly prepared room of the inn 'Stadt Frankfurt'. The stamina which we displayed during the weeks spent studying his extremely difficult vocal Mass [in E minor], which was performed at the official opening of the votive chapel of the new cathedral, showed the extent to which we loved our choirmaster. In the warm month of August, male and female singers patiently tolerated what must have been over twenty rehearsals in the stifling room, while Bruckner conducted in his shirt-sleeves.

[Auer, *Anton Bruckner, sein Leben und Werke*, 212–15]

LINDA SCHÖNBECK

Ferdinand Krackowizer's account gives a detailed picture of Bruckner as he must have appeared to many of his fellow citizens in his later years at Linz. Though it allows for slight oddities, it still represents the composer as a 'genuine, respectable, cheerful Upper Austrian' – a far cry from the bizarre eccentric of some of the better-known anecdotes. The following account is by a Linz woman who, like Krackowizer, sang under Bruckner, and apparently took part in the first performance of the E minor Mass. It suggests a somewhat odder character, and tells us a little more about Bruckner's susceptibility to young women.

There were two sides to Anton Bruckner.

In his private life he was always a child of nature – innocent, naïve, without malice, pleasant and obliging to everyone and more than modest.

However, he seems to have become aware of his artistic gifts early on. Despite his unbelievably poor background, the young Bruckner managed to make contact with eminent musicians, and through them to find the means of realizing his still dormant potential and educating himself further.

It was after he became Cathedral Organist at Linz that he was at last able to set his sights on advanced studies in harmony, and thus take another step towards the fulfilment of his deepest wishes. As I have said, his material resources were unfortunately not enough to sustain him through a full-time course of studies; above all, he still had to earn his daily bread.

Luckily the notion of luxury was completely alien to him. He was sober and undemanding in everything he did.

His clean-shaven classical face always bore a cheerful expression, his hair and moustache were cut short, and his ample form was never fashionably dressed.

In all the years that I knew the man, he always wore the same thing in summer: an unlined, black Orléans jacket, never buttoned up as he was always too hot; a pair of broad, shapeless breeches; a high-buttoned waistcoat; and either a straw or a slouch-hat of the most primitive kind. On particularly hot days he went about with the sleeves of his airy jacket always sticking out, his hat in one hand, in the other a huge, coloured handkerchief with which he wiped the sweat from his forehead.

When he was working on his compositions he would develop an almost nervous irritability. Naturally everything had to be worked out perfectly, and for Bruckner that meant down to the last detail.

He worked untiringly at attracting the best musicians, and Upper Austria supplied him with as many as it could. For this reason, Bruckner's works attained that splendour in performance that so impressed him in his model, his musical hero Richard Wagner.

The preparations for such a performance (in Linz, of course) were always very characteristic. Normally the rehearsal was announced for eight o'clock in the evening. We women singers would arrive on time, to find Bruckner already there. Not so the men! This got on Bruckner's nerves. On the stroke of eight he would set off in his shirt-sleeves, without hat or coat, to find the singers. Usually he would find them at 'Mayreder' (now 'Zain-inger', Franz-Josef-Platz) or in the 'Bairische Hof', at that time much-loved by singers. After he had given them a serious talking-to (naturally an object of fun amongst the less serious-minded), he drove his flock of singers back, panting and dripping with sweat, and now we could get down to work.

His enthusiasm was often tested, as it was only with some effort that he could keep the boisterous men of the choir on the right course after their visit to the tavern.

There was always a funny scene or two at these rehearsals, which often went on until around midnight. But success was assured, and Bruckner was encouraged to attempt further performances, despite the daunting problems that always arose.

His Mass [in E minor] was performed at the consecration of the chapel in the new Cathedral of the Immaculate Conception in Linz. It was prepared with such accuracy and splendour that Bruckner got the idea of chartering a steamboat and taking all the performers down the river to Vienna to perform the work.

I am not sure what prevented the project from being realized. I suspect that envy and resentment, in addition to the practical problems, played a major role; not surprisingly, given the interest shown in this outstanding composer by the capital's musical circles.

Bruckner's dealings with the 'eternal feminine' should not be taken too seriously, and it was lucky that women did not take him very seriously either. He played the suitor openly and unashamedly, but he was never touchy or indignant about any of his romantic failures, even though they often cost him a few tears at the time.

A short commentary on the above: while I was still at school, our singing-teacher, Alois Weinwurm (a brother of the once-famous Rudolf Weinwurm of Vienna), asked me and a young schoolmate if we would take part in a Credo by Bruckner at a service at the Parish Church in Linz. Having obtained permission from our Principal, we agreed, and since we both had good, true voices, my friend sang first soprano, and I, second; and so the addition of our strong, youthful voices ensured that the choral writing had its full effect. The rehearsal satisfied Bruckner completely (he was conducting), and on the next day the performance went ahead to general delight. At our next singing lesson our teacher handed my friend, on the composer's instruction, a love-song written by Bruckner, in which he opened his heart to the young girl – at that time she was barely sixteen. His affections, which he displayed in this lavish manner, were for the most part a complete surprise to the young lady concerned.

Once he went on a trip to Kirchdorf (with its charmingly situated market-place on the Pyhrnbahn, much loved by holiday-makers) with several friends – Bruckner had many. The trip took in the fortress at Altpernstein (an attractive ruin on a wooded hill, with lovely view along the valley towards the great hammer-forge and cement works). When they came to the dungeons, Bruckner crawled – or rather, squeezed – his way inside through a narrow hole in the wall. But when it came to getting back out again, all his efforts were in vain. No one knew what to do. The fearful Bruckner relived all the torments of the prisoners of olden times. And while he was experiencing these terrifying fantasies, he composed a *resurrexit*, until at last they were able to get his voluminous frame free.

[Gräflinger, 92–6]

II

THE MAN

A Child of Nature?

Ferdinand Krackowizer's and Linda Schönbeck's references to the 1869 first performance of the E minor Mass take us slightly beyond the date of Bruckner's decisive move to Vienna. Although the idea of going to Vienna seems to have been in Bruckner's mind for some time, it was only after his recovery from a serious nervous collapse in 1867 that he at last applied for posts at the Hofkapelle and at Vienna University. These applications were unsuccessful; but the following year Bruckner was offered a professorship at the Vienna Conservatory, in succession to his old teacher, Sechter. Typically, he had to be coerced into accepting the post. However, after some indecision he agreed, moving to Vienna with his sister Nani in the summer of 1868. Vienna was to be his home for the rest of his life, though the Viennese musical intelligentsia treated him very badly, subjecting him to such nightmarish humiliations as the première of the Third Symphony in 1877 (see pp. 111–16), and after that to several years of near-total neglect. Not surprisingly, Bruckner often felt the need to retreat to his Upper Austrian homeland, to St Florian or, in later years, to stay with friends in Steyr.

With Bruckner, a physical move usually accompanied a change in musical direction. After his arrival in Vienna, Bruckner wrote no more masses, concentrating his attention on the symphony. Of the nine numbered symphonies, all but No. 1 were written in Vienna, and it may be that the so-called 'Symphony No. 0' was also composed after the move from Linz; the only major religious works from the Viennese days are the *Te Deum* (1884) and *Psalm 150* (1892). The overwhelming majority of Bruckner reminiscences concern these Vienna days, especially the final twelve years (i.e. after the triumphant 1884 première of the Seventh Symphony in Leipzig), when Bruckner was at last beginning to experience something like the recognition he deserved. The nature of many of these recollections invites a thematic grouping – sections dealing in turn with different aspects of Bruckner's character and musicianship. Most of these aspects have already been identified or alluded to in the 'Vocation' section; it is now time to examine them in more detail.

FRITZ KREISLER

The virtuoso violinist Fritz Kreisler (1875–1962) entered the Vienna Conservatory at the unprecedentedly early age of seven. For three years, he studied violin with Joseph Hellmesberger and theory with Bruckner. His conversation with Louis Lochner about Bruckner (recorded in Lochner's book *Fritz Kreisler*) dates from much later. It is written in the form of an interview; I have simply removed the remarks not directly attributed to Kreisler. The tone of this recollection is very much in keeping with the romantic notion of Bruckner as a Parsifalian 'pure fool' – or in Linda Schönbeck's words, 'a child of nature'. Taking into account Bruckner's private Latin and legal studies (see above p. 14), plus his training as a high-school teacher, the reader is at liberty to doubt Kreisler's assertion that the composer 'knew almost nothing' beyond music and religion.

Anton Bruckner was combination of genius and simpleton. He had two co-ordinates – music and religion. Beyond that he knew almost nothing. I doubt whether he could multiply or subtract correctly.

Religion was very real with him. If the nearby bells tolled, he would either fall on his knees in the midst of a class lesson and pray or, more often, would leave us and rush over to the church for his devotions.

He was a man without guile and of a childlike naïvety. We youngsters, I must confess, took advantage of these traits of his. I recall two instances. One day, some sort of official imperial commission, headed, if my memory serves me right, by Professor Hermann von Helmholtz, dropped in on our class to see how Bruckner's pupils were doing. I may say parenthetically that Bruckner was not a good teacher, though he was a magnificent, exemplary human being.

To my amazement, the revered *Meister* asked me, as the youngest one in the class, to go to the blackboard and write something in fugue style. 'Fritz,' he said, 'compose a fugue quickly.' I was then only eight years old. I was flabbergasted. My mind was a blank. No theme would occur to me on the spur of the moment. But our teacher had given us a little textbook with about ninety themes for fugues composed by himself. I knew them by heart. I boldly wrote one of them on the blackboard. Bruckner, completely forgetting that he had composed and given them to us, looked at my product approvingly and observed. 'Not bad at all.'

My bluff had worked with Bruckner. Not, however, with my classmates, the youngest of whom were three years older than I. When class was dismissed, the boys waited for me outside and gave me a sound thrashing. They were so comradely, however, as not to give me away to the *Meister* . . .

Bruckner had a chubby, fat pug dog named Mops.* He would leave us with Mops munching our sandwiches while he himself hastened off to luncheon. We decided we'd play a joke on our teacher which would flatter him. So while the *Meister* was away, we'd play a motif by Wagner, and as we did so, would slap Mops and chase him. Next we'd start Bruckner's *Te Deum*, and while this music was in progress, would give Mops something to eat. He soon showed a convincing preference for the *Te Deum*! When we thought we had trained him sufficiently so that he would automatically run away when Wagner was played and joyfully approach us at the sound of a Bruckner strain, we deemed the moment appropriate for our prank.

'Meister Bruckner,' we said one day as he returned from lunch, 'we know that you are devoted to Wagner, but to our way of thinking he cannot compare with you. Why even a dog would know that you are a greater composer than Wagner.'

Our guileless teacher blushed. He thought we were serious. He reproved us, paid tribute to Wagner as unquestionably the greatest contemporary, but was nevertheless filled with enough curiosity to ask what we meant by claiming even a dog could tell the difference.

This was the moment we had waited for. We played a Wagner motif. A howling, scared Mops stole out of the room. We started

*The anecdote is priceless; however the author has been unable to find any other references to Bruckner owning a dog, with or without the name 'Mops'.

in on Bruckner's *Te Deum*. A happy canine returned, wagging his tail and pawing expectantly at our sleeves. Bruckner was touched.

[Louis P. Lochner, *Fritz Kreisler*, 9–11]

FELIX VON KRAUS

The Vienna-born bass Felix von Kraus (1870–1937) was noted for his *Lieder* and oratorio performances. As a student, he attended Bruckner's harmony classes at Vienna University, but his first encounter with the composer occurred somewhat earlier. Kraus's memories of Bruckner were collected and published, along with reminiscences of Brahms and Cosima Wagner, by his daughter Felicitas; the Bruckner stories make touching reading. The 'childlike' side of Bruckner's nature again emerges strikingly, with the added implication that the child of nature was at his happiest when surrounded by other children.

In the summer of 1884 we came to Vöcklabruck in Upper Austria, on the recommendation of my uncle. We stayed at Frau Forsthuber's guest-house in the market-place. Apart from us, the only other guest was an apparently very friendly old gentleman whom we saw every day at lunch and at dinner. At first the relationship did not progress beyond the customary exchange of greetings before and after meals. But things changed a few days later – the first rainy day. In the afternoon I wanted to enjoy a little private music-making with my brother in the lounge, where there was a piano. To our annoyance, however, we found the old gentleman there, enjoying his coffee. After a little hesitation, we went in and asked if it would disturb him if we played something. 'Oh, not at all,' he said kindly, 'I'm a musician too!' He listened to us, then after a little while he got up from his table and sat with us at the piano. Naturally we asked him if he was also a pianist. When he said yes, we asked him to play a sonata for us, and received another positive reply. After only the first few bars it was obvious to us that we 'artists' had been making fools of ourselves in front of a real Master – even though excessive modesty wasn't exactly one of our more striking qualities. When he came to the end of the movement, we thanked him and prepared to creep embarrassedly away, but it was impossible: the unknown genius wanted to go on playing, and it obviously gave him pleasure to watch us overcoming our shyness and enjoying the music, just as anybody would who had heard Anton Bruckner playing the piano or the organ – for this, of course, was who my partner at the piano was. Before dinner, he introduced himself to the other members of my family, and for the rest of the week he sat with us at the table at every meal-time, and went walking and swimming with us children. It amused us enormously when he jumped from the diving-board and made the small but very full pool overflow. After dinner there was always music, and he particularly enjoyed playing for us young people (children!) as we danced, which he did tirelessly.

On rainy days when we were alone with him, he would play duos with violin, or sit alone at the piano, playing whatever we wanted for as long as we wanted.

One day he airily invited us to give him a theme, so that he could see 'what he could do with it'. The variations he improvised left such an overwhelming impression that from then on we asked him continually to create free fantasies for us, and in his touchingly kind way he never tired of granting our wishes. The only thing he asked of us in return was that should go up with him to his room at bedtime and look in every cupboard and every corner, and shine our candles under the bed, so that he could be sure that no burglar was there in hiding. And so, evening after evening, we escorted him in solemn procession, with the two burning piano candles, performing our modest role conscientiously, reverently and thankfully. Our enthusiasm was based solely on the effect of his playing, because at the time the name Anton Bruckner meant absolutely nothing; neither the man nor a note of his music were known to us. In our excuse I should say that we were sixteen and thirteen and a half years old and understandably not regular concert-goers, and that this was 1884 when Bruckner was far from well known outside Viennese musical circles.

We move on ten years to 1894, the year Kraus attained his doctorate in musicology. His daughter tells us that he was helping Brahms's friend Eusebius Mandyczewski with corrections to 'a scholarly work' when the doorbell rang urgently. It was a messenger from the Gesellschaft der Musikfreunde. Half an hour before the public rehearsal of Bruckner's F minor Mass a message had been received from Court opera-singer Reichenberg: the bass part of the Mass – which he had only just seen for the first time – was too difficult for him; and so they had sent for Kraus to ask him if he would sing it at sight. When Kraus arrived at the Musikverein he found the audience noisily restless and the committee in despair, though no one was more desperate than the composer himself. A member of the Directorate, the laryngologist Professor Schrötter, took Kraus aside and told him that this was probably the last opportunity the seriously ill composer would have to hear his own work. Kraus agreed to sing. The narrative continues in his own words.

When I returned to my dressing-room, Bruckner ran towards me and wept happily like a little child. Before I could stop him, he kissed both my hands again and again and sobbed, 'Oh, my dear sir, I've only you to thank. That you've done this for me! I don't know how I can ever repay you for this!' I replied that in all honesty it was not necessary; it was I that should be repaying him. 'Why's that, then?' he asked. 'I don't know you and I've never done anything for you!' And so I asked him if he remembered a certain summer in Vöcklabruck at Frau Forsthuber's guest-house? 'Of course,' he replied, 'but what's that got to do with it?' 'Well,' I replied, 'perhaps you remember two teenage boys for whom you played so much music, and whose dancing you so kindly accompanied in the evenings? I was the younger of the two, and I am only too happy to have the opportunity to show my thanks at last!' His astonishment and childlike joy were truly touching. Immediately he remembered every small detail, and he revelled in the memory of that beautiful summer with all the warm nostalgia of one whose days are numbered; it was as though he had suddenly been transported back to those times of health and happiness. With tears in his eyes he folded his hands and said, 'Oh God, you move in mysterious ways!'

[Kraus, 15–17; 18–19]

FRIEDRICH KLOSE

In 1886, the German-born composer Friedrich Klose (1862–1942) came to Vienna to study privately with Bruckner, having previously received a 'general' education at Geneva University. He became a member of Bruckner's circle of young friends and admirers – Bruckner himself referred to them as his 'Gaudeamus'. In later years, Klose too was a noted composition teacher, first in Basel (1906), then in Munich (1907–19). His book, *Meine Lehrjahre bei Bruckner* ('My years of study with Bruckner') is primarily autobiographical, though it opens with a long and richly detailed description of the older composer, as man, musician and teacher. The following observations occur during a lengthy account of Bruckner's teaching methods. Klose's Bruckner is a more complicated being than Fritz Kreisler's 'combination of genius and simpleton', but his portrait tends to endorse Kreisler's assertion that the composer knew nothing beyond his 'two co-ordinates – music and religion'.

Sometimes, when I asked the Master to look at a piece of work I had newly finished, he would remain absolutely still, leaning well back in his chair, and pay no attention to my request. At first, I supposed he was thinking deeply about one of his compositions, but with time I realized that this always happened when the bell of the nearby Votivekirche sounded: Bruckner was praying. As soon as he had finished his short devotion, he would turn to me again, without my having to remind him, and look over my work.

Bruckner was a strict Catholic; there was no aesthetic or poetic inclination attached to his belief, only unshakeable faith in the Church, the almighty power, wisdom and goodness of his God, and the promise of a better life to come. This complete, resigned trust in providence was surely to blame for the lack of any urge to educate himself in scientific or any other kind of extra-musical matters; but it is very doubtful whether he would have been able to follow his *via dolorosa* so triumphantly to its end, without stumbling once, if he had not had that unwavering faith in divine providence and justice as his firm support. That faith and Church were purely private affairs for Bruckner was evident from the absolute tolerance which he showed towards those with other beliefs. Nothing that he said betrayed the slightest desire to influence anyone else in religious matters. And the following remark, one that I myself heard, proves that denominational considerations did not impair the impartiality of his judgement. He observed that, in his experience, those of his students who were Protestants applied themselves with more energy and diligence than the Catholics.

As I have already mentioned, Bruckner had hardly any intellectual needs. During my three-and-a-half student years, I knew of only three books and one pamphlet that he read – though he read them several times:

1. A work (I can no longer remember which) on the Mexican War, whose account of the fate of the tragic Emperor Maximilian moved him deeply.
2. A description of the Expedition to the North Pole on the ship *Tegetthoff*.
3. A small picture-book with biographies of Haydn, Mozart and Beethoven.
4. A kind of tract: 'The Miraculous Mary of Lourdes'.

It may at first seem curious that Bruckner should have bothered himself with books such as the first two; however, we can safely assume that his interest was not scientific but completely childlike, just as when we are young we find descriptions of great fires, criminal acts and other sensational things deliciously exciting. At the same time, this was coupled with a genuine, warm fellow-feeling in Bruckner, which must explain why in one of our earliest sessions the Master asked me for my own thoughts on the Mexican War and the death of Maximilian.

[Klose, 96–8]

CARL HRUBY

Like Friedrich Klose, the Viennese writer on music Carl Hruby (1869–1940) was a member of Bruckner's 'Gaudeamus'. He studied with Bruckner at the Conservatory.

His *Meine Erinnerungen an Anton Bruckner* ('My recollections of Anton Bruckner') is a short but fascinating book, saltily written and full of surprises – for instance, this snippet of Brucknerian table-talk.

On the subjects of religion and the Christian faith, Bruckner expressed himself more candidly and dispassionately than one would have expected from such a deeply pious man. On one occasion, when a large company of us were conversing on our pet subjects, the conversation came round by chance to religion, the hereafter and other eternal riddles of human existence. At one point – I've no idea how it came about – someone brought up the subject of David Strauss and his *Leben Jesu*,* and to my complete astonishment I discovered that Bruckner had read it. My amazement increased when I heard how calmly and objectively Bruckner spoke about this work. It was always risky to venture into conversation with Bruckner about such things; one could end up ruining one's relationship with him for good. One of our circle, however, asked the daring question as to whether Bruckner was convinced that there was life after death with eternal rewards and punishments, and (as if that wasn't enough) if he actually believed in the miraculous effectiveness of prayer. Bruckner's response was unexpectedly amusing: 'I'll tell you this: if it's true, all the better for me; if it isn't true, then praying won't do me any harm.' Truly, a perfect example of speculative Christianity: he wanted to be insured against every eventuality!

[Hruby, 38–9]

Bruckner, a speculative Christian? Carl Hruby isn't the only writer to suggest that Bruckner's religious attitudes were more complex than was commonly supposed: see, for instance, the account of his last months by Dr Richard Heller (p. 171–7). The following recollection also raises doubts about the popular image of Bruckner as inspired simpleton.

*David Strauss's *Das Leben Jesu* ('The Life of Jesus', 1836) was a pioneering critique of the Gospel narratives. At the time Hruby knew Bruckner, the book was still deeply controversial – certainly not the kind of thing a strict, old-fashioned Catholic would have been expected to read.

MAX VON MILLENKOVICH-MOROLD

At the time of his acquaintance with Bruckner, Max von Millenkovich-Morold (1866–1945) was a law student. From 1898, he was a ministerial secretary at the Ministry of Education; then in 1917 he held the post of Director of the Burgtheater for a year. He was also known as a writer, under the name 'Morold'.

I got to know Bruckner personally in my youth (during the 1880s) in the Academic Wagner Sociey of Vienna and in Bayreuth. As a very young, insignificant person who belonged to completely different circles from Bruckner's own group of friends, I naturally did not know him 'intimately'; rather, I observed him from a distance and heard more *about* him than from him directly. One thing is nevertheless certain: if he had been in some way *strange*, then precisely because I was young and not on 'intimate' terms with him, I would definitely have noticed; and if he had appeared strange or peculiar to most other people, who knew him more closely, then I would without doubt have heard about it and my attention and curiosity would certainly have been aroused. However, I remember *nothing* of the sort. Furthermore, the detailed letters which I sent to my parents about the people whom I knew then, my artistic impressions, etc. (I am still in possession of these and they provide an invaluable source for reviving my memory), express – despite only hesitant familiarity with Bruckner's music – *only* the deepest admiration for Bruckner the man, or tremendous respect for Bruckner the professor. For me this is conclusive evidence that the 'hulking', 'boorish' and even unintelligent (!) Bruckner is a later invention. Not even his wide trousers succeeded in irritating me.

[Göllerich/Auer, 4/2, 12]

ALEXANDER FRÄNKEL

Some of the most intriguing remarks on the subject of Bruckner's intellectual capabilities come from the surgeon Alexander Fränkel (1857–1941). Fränkel was part of a group of young medics that used to meet at the inn, 'Riedhof', to which Bruckner was introduced by a fellow Upper Austrian, Karl Rabl. He was soon accepted as an honorary member, playing, in Fränkel's words, 'sometimes an active, sometimes a passive role'. While admitting Bruckner's 'unusual simplicity', Fränkel also allows us a glimpse of a lively, inquisitive intellect.

As a frequent guest at our table, Bruckner was almost embarrassingly modest towards us: time and time again he felt it necessary to stress the fact that he considered it a great honour for a 'poor musician' to be received by such 'learned' men in such a kind, considerate and friendly manner. He would listen to our medical conversations with eager attention and a touching, compassionate interest in the people whose medical conditions, operations, etc., we were discussing. He would return to them repeatedly in conversation and never grew tired of asking questions in order to keep up to date on the condition of the patients – joyfully moved if he received good news, deeply upset if he discovered that the art of medicine had failed. It went so far that we had to spare his feelings by keeping some sad truths from him. When Bruckner sought medical instruction he would not be satisfied with superficial information; he wanted to be taught thoroughly, and often required illustrations, particularly if the information was anatomical. The insight into the structure of the human body which he gained in this way opened up a whole new world to him, one of which he had previously known nothing. He showed the liveliest interest in our discussions, even when they were of a particularly scientific nature, and he would make sure that we explained things to him. But this was not all: Bruckner was able to absorb information from all fields of knowledge, and because he already considered us his learned Areopagus we were often called upon to answer, as best we could, questions which he had drawn from the most diverse branches of contemporary intellectual thought. At the time I knew him, electrical engineering was experiencing its first boom, and I myself was granted the honour of serving as his cicerone at the first Electrical Exhibition. I tried, where possible, to use the exhibits to explain the phenomena, according to my very limited understanding of the subject. It cannot be denied that Bruckner possessed only a very modest amount of what is generally termed 'education'. As far as education is synonymous with specific learning, the course of his development shows that he could not have received a great deal. However, anyone who knew him better quickly realized his mental potential and the adaptability of his intellect. Admittedly he was not a bookworm; but whatever the outside world gave him he took in with great ease, plus anything else he could learn peripatetically. Even if the sum of all the knowledge which he carried around in his head was not very great, his intelligence was well above average. The oddity of his outward appearance was immediately noticeable, as was his unusual simplicity, modesty and truthfulness. Through further contact with him, one became aware of the high artistic goals this simple man strove to attain, for their own sake, as though it were as a matter of course. He did not hesitate to apply all his strength, nor did he ever despair completely. Greatness was manifest in this man as an entirely natural, innate function of an organism which had been predetermined for this function.

[Göllerich/Auer, 4/2, 20–23]

Wide Trousers and Kid Gloves

Sympathetic as he seems to Bruckner, Alexander Fränkel concedes the 'oddity of his outward appearance', and there is evidence that the Riedhof circle may have made more of this than Fränkel admits (see August Stradal, p. 48). Many of Bruckner's acquaintances describe some kind of eccentricity, especially those who knew him in later years. In the next extract, a friend recalls his first encounter with Bruckner, and gives an idea of his reputation in Vienna in the late 1870s.

FRIEDRICH ECKSTEIN

Publicist, philosopher, industrialist, amateur musician – Friedrich Eckstein (1861–1939) was a spectacular example of a Viennese dilettante. He left valuable reminiscences of Bruckner in two books: *Erinnerungen an Anton Bruckner* ('Recollections of Anton Bruckner'), largely an account of Bruckner's theoretical values and teaching methods, and the autobiographical *Alte unnennbare Tage!* ('Old, unnameable days' – a line from the poet Eduard Mörike), which offers a fuller portrait of Bruckner as man and artist. Eckstein studied with Bruckner at the Conservatory from 1880, and privately from 1884. In later years he helped the composer financially, covering most of the costs of the publication of the *Te Deum*. The disastrous Bruckner performance Eckstein refers to was the première of the Third Symphony in 1877.

I still vividly remember the moment I first set eyes on the strange figure of Anton Bruckner, even though it happened almost six decades ago. It was a beautiful autumn morning in the year 1879, and I was just approaching the Josephsplatz, talking animatedly with a friend, a certain Kapellmeister. We had just arrived at the narrow passageway between the Spanish Riding School and the Redoutensaal when we saw coming towards us a rather stout, darkly attired old gentleman. He responded to my companion's greeting with a bow, in the process lowering his black, wide-brimmed felt hat almost to the ground. This gesture allowed me a glimpse of the top of his huge, close-shaven head, which, during the following conversation, he frequently wiped with an enormous blue silk handkerchief. Smiling, he made a few friendly remarks, described a conversation with Director Hellmesberger, offered us his snuff-box, tapped it carefully, took a pinch for himself and, with the residue dangling from his moustache, went on his way with a friendly wave.

'That's Professor Anton Bruckner,' said my friend. 'They don't come much odder, and people's opinions of him are sharply divided. He teaches harmony and counterpoint at the Conservatory; I've attended his lectures myself. He also teaches at the University, and he's rightly considered a leading theorist. As for his compositions, I get the impression that nobody really knows what to make of them. Some are pretty damning, but there's also a small group of musicians who see him as one of the great Masters.' My companion felt unable to judge from his own experience as he had never had the opportunity to hear a single note of Bruckner. Nothing of his had been performed for years, probably because the last time a Bruckner work had been played in public the audience had fled the hall in droves and the critics had been completely mystified. But on this everyone was agreed: that Bruckner was a magnificent organist, that in fact he was without equal in that field, especially when it came to improvisation.

[Eckstein, *Alte unnennbare Tage!*, 137–8]

'They don't come much odder,' says Friedrich Eckstein's Kapellmeister friend. His inability to know what to make of Bruckner may, as he says, be partly explained by circumstances, but it also seems to reflect something paradoxical in the man himself; an unnamed Viennese wit summed up Bruckner as 'half Caesar, half peasant'. The next reminiscence opens with a very similar image.

RICHARD HELLER

Dr Richard Heller was one of two physicians who looked after Bruckner during his last years. Heller began visiting the composer in the winter of 1894, when Bruckner was recovering from a serious attack of pleurisy. Most of his generously detailed report is given at the end of the book, but the details about Bruckner's wardrobe and general personal appearance are more appropriate here. Old and sick though he was, Bruckner seems to have clung to his old habits of dress and scrupulous cleanliness for as long as he could. Heller also introduces another important character: Bruckner's housekeeper, Katharina ('Kathi') Kachelmayr. More of her later.

No one who saw Bruckner could ever forget the impression made by that characteristic head, reminiscent of a cinquecento bust, in combination with his almost comical physique.

The resemblance between that striking profile and the head of a Roman emperor was strengthened by his constant refusal to wear a beard, and by his habit of cropping his thick, white hair almost to the skull. His body was small and thick-set. His feet were shod in broad, almost rectangular sealskin ankle boots, with a kind of crease across the instep (he owned about thirty pairs of these shoes). Above these, he wore a pair of immensely wide, bag-like trousers. His jackets were of similar expanse and each one had its own name, so the faithful Kathi needed a good memory if she was always to bring the right one. One of them was called 'Shaggy' because it was made of thick Loden material; another was 'the Cords' since this one was made of worsted; a third was 'the Dandy', or 'the Bobby', or 'Fatty'; and so on. His hats were also given names. The 'Hüadal' (a little hat) was the one he usually wore, a black, broad-brimmed slouch-hat; his Sunday hat was simply 'The Hat'; while 'The Top Hat' was a collapsible opera hat of prehistoric design, which he put on only for very special ceremonious occasions. The basic principal of his wardrobe was spacious and comfortable – a principal which he carried to grotesque lengths.

His way of living was as simple as he himself was, and anyone who saw the Master slurping up his soup from the bowl would have thought that he was in the company of a farm-hand grown old in honourable service rather than a great composer.

Even in old age he was scrupulously clean, putting on a fresh shirt and soft collar every day – having thoroughly washed himself – and he was disconsolate if anyone arrived before he was fully dressed up. He would wait for me in full attire, with a black necktie (which he always tied himself), sitting in the armchair. After his serious illness he had given up smoking and now took snuff in considerable quantities. Two snuff-boxes stood at the ready: a silver one for himself, and a gold one filled with the 'Divine Blend' for visitors.

[Karl Kobald (ed.), *In Memoriam Anton Bruckner*, 24–5]

SEPP STÖGER

Both Friedrich Eckstein and Richard Heller draw attention to Bruckner's close-shaven head; the apparently widespread belief (deriving from photographs and portraits) that the composer was bald is mistaken. Sepp Stöger (1869–1938) was a barber from the town of Steyr in Upper Austria, who later became known as a dialect poet. He cut Bruckner's hair regularly when the composer came to stay at the presbytery in Steyr during the summer holidays. As Stöger reveals, Bruckner took great pains about his hair, and with his moustache, evidently believing that the results made him more socially presentable. Stöger tells us that Bruckner used to send for him three times a week!

It is not widely known that Dr Bruckner wore a moustache. It was not allowed to be more than a finger wide and was always trimmed very short with a pair of scissors. it was his 'Salonbärtchen', a moustache for mixing in cultured and intellectual society. He often said that this was the name which Princess Valerie, his most admired patron, gave to his pencil moustache. He also wore his hair in a peculiar style, unlike almost anyone else in the world. 'Next time you can cut my hair,' he once ordered, 'but make it short, as short as you can.' At that time the American haircuttingmachines were a particular novelty. On seeing that I was about to use one for my work of art, Bruckner was outraged and asked what I was doing. 'Cutting your hair with a machine!' I replied. 'I can't stand that, it makes me nervous, I want it done with ordinary scissors,' he cried. Obediently I picked up the scissors and comb in order to cut his hair *à la Fiesko*, but once again it wasn't right for him. 'What are you doing there now? I said very short!' he shouted indignantly. Then he explained to me that he wanted his hair cut off right next to the scalp, without a comb. It still amazes me today that the Master, who was otherwise such a nervous person, enjoyed this. I gave the task a full hour of my time. Whilst I was cutting he told me about the vicious music critic Hanslick and others of his opponents; about his splendid success abroad, at the Crystal Palace in London and in Paris. Somewhere an enthusiastic crowd had once unharnessed the horses and pulled his carriage themselves. 'As for my own countrymen,' he often complained, 'they won't realize what I can do till I'm dead. It's always like that here.' A score covered with an enormous amount of notes always lay on his piano. When, concerned, I asked him if later somebody would be able to read his scribblings, he laughed and assured me that this would certainly be the case. He paid me what was then the princely sum of a silver guilder for cutting his hair. As I was picking up the fallen hair and wrapping it up in paper he asked, 'What on earth are you doing there?' 'I'm picking it up!' I replied. Laughing, he patted me on the shoulder: 'You're an idiot, but you're right, perhaps one day some fool'll give you a hundred guilders for it.'

[Göllenrich/Auer, 4/3, 169–70]

ROSA PAPIER-PAUMGARTNER

Bruckner was never more concerned about his appearance than when he was keeping company with women. Rosa Papier-Paumgartner (1858–1932) was a member of the Vienna Hofoper until throat problems brought her career to a premature end in 1891. She advised Bruckner on who to chose for the solo parts in the first performance of the *Te Deum*. In this article she recalls the first time Bruckner presented himself at her home.

Anton Bruckner was a dear friend of our household. I remember his first visit quite clearly. I had taken over the alto solo in one of his choral compositions and he came to thank me officially. He climbed the steps slowly, stopping half-way up to struggle with the new kid gloves which he had put on in my honour. The housekeeper had noticed him fumbling with his gloves. He told her that he was looking for the Kammersängerin Papier-Paumgartner; she showed him our apartment and then went up ahead of him in order to announce his visit: 'A certain Herr Bruckner's coming, and he's struggling ever so much with his gloves.' My husband and I met him on the staircase. Bruckner raised his hat and kissed my hand. 'Madam Kammersängerin . . .' he began, still fiddling with his gloves, which he could not get over the back of his hands. We did not let him finish but took him by the arm and led him into our apartment. 'First of all, Master,' I said to him, 'take off those awkward gloves.' His embarrassment disappeared with his gloves and he spoke freely and casually; we had a stimulating afternoon. Later he visited us much more frequently; he was a kind, inwardly deeply emotional person.

[*Tagespost*, Linz, 21 September 1928]

FRIEDRICH KLOSE

Friedrich Klose now gives a characteristically entertaining account of his first visit to Bruckner in Vienna. It shows that, however much Bruckner may have worried about his own appearance, décor was a matter of rather less importance. Klose offers insight into another of Bruckner's apparent eccentricities, his preference for 'old-fashioned' candle-light.

Having successfully concluded my search for accommodation, I made my way to Bruckner. He lived at Number 7, Hessgasse, opposite the Sühnhaus, erected on the site of the burnt-out Ringtheater. With a pounding heart, I climbed the four flights of stairs and, after some hesitation, rang the doorbell – it was a glass door, with a metal grille and green curtains. All was quiet. I breathed a sigh of relief: for how would my confidence, which tended to shrink at even small challenges, survive the vital test of whether I was cut out to be a musician? The thought that Bruckner might not be at home encouraged me to ring once more. This time, there were sounds of movement. With perhaps a hint of reluctance, I noted footsteps quickly drawing nearer and the swishing back of the green curtain, and then I recognized Bruckner, peering out from behind the grille with a none too kindly expression on his face. The door was opened, and as I began, stammeringly, 'Herr Professor, I'm sure you don't remember me . . .' Bruckner's expression brightened, and with the words, 'Ah yes, Herr Klose from Bayreuth,' he extended his hand warmly towards me. He was busy composing just now, he said, but perhaps I might come in for a moment. Never in my wildest dreams had I expected such an encouraging reception, or presumed that the Master would have retained such a vivid memory of me four years after our meeting in Bayreuth.

From the anteroom – where the gloom and the long, looping wreaths that hung from the walls reminded me rather more of a burial chamber – via the housekeeper's room, we came at last to Bruckner's study. I will never forget the impression this strange, cell-like room made on me as I went in. The first thing that struck me was an old yellow-brown grand piano almost in the middle of the room, the keyboard open, with manuscripts lying on the music-stand. On the lid, sheets of music and a substantial part of Bruckner's wardrobe lay cosily together. Near one of the two windows opposite the entrance (the one on the right, to be precise) stood the work-table, a very simple rectangular piece of furniture; the top – where it was not covered by documents, music-sheets and newspapers – was stained black with ink and marked with Bruckner's notes in chalk. The corner by the left window was filled by an enormous square box: the harmonium. A chest-of-drawers, a plain iron bed and a wash-stand completed the modest furnishings. The room was of an appropriately comfortable size for one of these new, purpose-built, Viennese rented apartments. What made it so strange was the colour of the walls, which from the floor to the ceiling were painted in a loud, gaudy blue, which reminded me of the little blue balls used in the wash . . .

I spent the time before my first official lesson in a mixture of high excitement and dread. I made a careful selection of the work I had done with my teachers Lachner and Ruthardt, and added several independent compositions, amongst them my recently performed orchestral symphonic poem *Loreley*, and made my way again to Bruckner – this was on 3 February 1886. As on my first visit, it was Bruckner himself who answered the door. This time his study seemed completely transformed. From that first morning's meeting, I had retained a rather fond memory of that room with its enormous windows; but now, by the light of two candles which burned brightly on the ink-stained desk and threw quivering shadows on the walls, it seemed the perfect setting for an inquisition. As I waited for the awful judgement, I seemed to see the shape of a death's head between the two flickering lights.

The reason why the Master used such old-fashioned lighting was fear of fire. This fear stemmed from the great conflagration, just across the street from Bruckner's rooms, which had reduced the Ringtheater to ashes and taken hundreds of lives. When the fire broke out, Bruckner was near the old University, where he saw the blaze lighting up the skies and learned the Ringtheater was in flames. Seized with unspeakable dread for the fate of his manuscripts, he rushed desperately home. An enormous crowd had built up on the Ring. The breathless composer found his way barred by the police. Luckily, an acquaintance wearing a medal ribbon was able to persuade them to let him through, and Bruckner stormed up the four staircases to his apartment. With feverish haste, he threw together his life's work, his very heart's blood – for us today, one of the most exalted of all artistic treasures – in case the raging element should spread further. This terrible experience was the cause of the fear that compelled Bruckner to stick with the seemingly less dangerous candle-light. Anyone with a decent imagination would not find it strange, let alone funny, that the Master usually extinguished candles with moistened fingers instead of blowing them out, nor that after leaving the room he would come back once more and peer into the darkness to see if any tiny spark might still be burning in the wick.

[Klose, 9–13]

So far, the Brucknerian eccentricities described in this section have been fairly mild – good material for what several of the writers in this volume have described as 'amusing' or 'touching' anecdotes. What follows is rather different.

KARL WALDECK

Karl Waldeck got to know Bruckner well while he was working as an assistant teacher in Linz. He became a pupil of Bruckner, and was later his successor as organist at Linz cathedral, on Bruckner's own recommendation. Interestingly, Waldeck also mentions a ritual with candle-light; but the observations in paragraph two are rather more striking. Waldeck blames overwork for Bruckner's obsessional behaviour; this must be partly true, but compare his explanation with that of Max von Oberleithner (p. 46), who – significantly – also links the Kyrie of the Mass in F minor with Bruckner's state of mind during the 1866–7 crisis.

When Bruckner improvised at the piano, the candle always had to be extinguished. I also had to play my own attempts at composition, for which I always earned his praise. Once, when we were talking about the effort needed to be able to improvise on such a high thematic and contrapuntal level, Bruckner said, 'If one day you come to write my biography, you can say that at St Florian I used to practise for ten hours at the piano and three at the great organ almost every day, and that my musical studies would then last well into the night.' Given the extra strain on the nerves caused by organ improvisation, which on big instruments demands both formidable technique and great physical effort, Bruckner feared that in later years the duties of an organist would become too much for him; and as he had no success with private tuition he worried that in old age he would waste away on a salary of just

500 florins. Bruckner also realized that as a composer it was better for him to remain in one of the bigger cities. All this made him decide to prepare himself for examination with Sechter, which he finally sat after spending several hours with Sechter every day for week after week; and yet in the end his contrapuntal improvisation impressed the examination committee more than all his theoretical learning. The pile of notepaper that he covered with work for Sechter would have reached from the floor to the underside of the piano.

Despite his powerful physique and his 'healthy appetite', Bruckner was unable to avoid the consequences of such over-exertion. His mental balance was disturbed and he suffered terribly from depression, obsessions, etc. For example, while out walking one day, he halted in front of a tree to count the leaves. Once he walked into my lodgings without knocking or saying a word in greeting, sat down at the piano and played for a while. When I asked him what he was playing, he said, 'The Kyrie of my new F minor Mass.' In company, his condition usually led to general merriment, but I felt sorry for him and stayed with him as much as possible, and when I came to take my leave of him late into the night he would beg me to stay, for if he was left to himself he would be tormented by his obsessions again. For the rest of his life, Bruckner was grateful to me for standing by him during the most painful period of his life – as is obvious from his letters. He also promised me that if, as he deserved, he was made Court Kapellmeister, he would bring me to Vienna as Court Organist.

Although Bruckner's health was improved by the water-treatment at Kreuzen (near Grein, Upper Austria), he retained – aside from a servility towards his superiors (who were very familiar towards their organist) – many strange characteristics, especially a certain thoughtlessness in his behaviour towards his best friends, which his enemies used to cast doubt on his sanity and musicality. I once read this remark, 'As an organist, Bruckner is a complete amateur and his compositions are madness.'

[Gräflinger, 114–16]

MAX VON OBERLEITHNER

Max von Oberleithner recalls the composer early in 1890, again showing signs of what Linda Schönbeck called 'nervous irritability'. The second version of the Eighth Symphony was complete, but Bruckner was feeling neglected, and he was just beginning his obsessionally meticulous revision of the First Symphony.

This was not an artistically productive time for Bruckner, and his ill humour meant that it was not easy to get conversation flowing in the evenings, especially as I was just twenty-one years old, and daily news or theatrical events held no interest at all for him. Only once was his curiosity awakened, when a dreadful murder was reported in the papers, and he probed me for details which naturally I could not provide. A discussion about music, in particular our shared enthusiasm for Wagner, might have been the most obvious recourse; however, when a composer has spent all day working at musical problems, one should not burden his brain with the same theme in the evening, and when on one occasion I laid stress on the ethical significance of Wagner's poetry, he referred me to the end of the first act of *Walküre* . . .*

[Oberleithner, 32–3]

AUGUST STRADAL

August Stradal (1860–1930) studied with Bruckner at the Vienna Conservatory and then, from 1883, privately. A fine pianist (he also was a pupil of Liszt), he made solo piano arrangements of Symphonies 1, 2, 5, 6 and 8. If the 'young, jovial doctors' Stradal mentions are (as seems likely) Alexander Fränkel's circle, this throws a rather different light on parts of the latter's narrative. In the previous extract, Max von Oberleithner recalled only one example of Bruckner's hunger for news of a 'dreadful murder'; in Stradal's experience, it was clearly habitual.

*Bruckner is obviously thinking of the incestuous love of Siegmund and Sieglinde – not quite what Oberleithner means by 'ethical significance'.

Bruckner devoured such news with nervous greed, and often it was not enough for him to have merely the special supplement; sometimes I had to bring him half-a-dozen newspapers in which there was a report of some sensational affair. Of course, every paper said just about the same thing, but Bruckner read through every report on a case which interested him, word for word. If there was to be a trial of a murderer or an execution, then for days beforehand Bruckner was unable to sleep, due to his excitement.

For example, when the trial of the infamous murderer of women, Hugo Schenk, began, Bruckner pleaded with me to speak to my friend the public prosecutor, Gürtler von Kleeborn, an arrange permission for Bruckner to attend the trial and if possible the execution. Finally, after much hard work, I succeeded in talking him out of the latter, but I still had to gain him entry into the courtroom, in which the most horrible tragedies of life had their conclusion. He kept asking me what the defendant had said, often jumped up from the bench to get a better view of the murderer and generally disturbed the peace until a court official came over and ordered the Master to be silent. The evening before Schenk's execution, we had supper in the 'Riedhof', a restaurant close by the district court. With us there were several young, jovial doctors, who of course knew nothing of Bruckner's greatness. To my anger they began to tease the 'peculiar old man'. One of the young men told us that Hugo Schenk's last wish had been to eat a schnitzel from the 'Riedhof' on the eve of his execution, adding that the landlord had just sent one over to the district court. Immediately Bruckner asked the landlord to prepare him a schnitzel from the same piece of veal as the one which had been given to Schenk. Bruckner then stayed up the whole night and prayed for the murderer.

[Göllerich/Auer, 4/2, 567–8]

Bruckner and Women

Some of the strangest Bruckner stories centre on his relationships with women – or, one should say, young women: most of the objects of Bruckner's desire were scarcely past girlhood. Ferdinand Krackowizer and Linda Schönbeck have already told us something about Bruckner's infatuations. Krackowizer notes that 'the object of Bruckner's admiration never remained the same for any great length of time'. If anything, that errs on the side of understatement, as this first collection of stories shows.

FRANZ GRÄFLINGER

Franz Gräflinger (1876–1962) studied and later taught at the Linz Musikverein School. His book *Anton Bruckner – Bausteine zu seiner Lebensgeschichte* ('Anton Bruckner – building blocks for his life-story') brings together recollections, mostly of the younger Bruckner, several of which are incorporated in this book. The following account is not first-hand: Gräflinger summarizes stories told by Karl Waldeck, the organist friend who described Bruckner's counting neuroses during his 1866–7 breakdown. The material is, nevertheless, indispensable. Gräflinger's final remark is intriguing: it certainly runs counter to most verdicts on Bruckner as love object.

Bruckner's oddity is well illustrated by this little love-story. In Linz, one girl made a particularly strong impression on the ever-susceptible Bruckner. Every day in May, the young woman went to the evening service at the church, so Bruckner did the same, positioning himself close to her. A few days later he invited the girl's parents, whom he knew, to make a family outing to St Florian to hear the great organ. After this first approach, Bruckner decided that the next step was to offer the girl a gift. He presented himself at the family house and handed the maid a present for the young lady – a prayer-book. One can imagine Bruckner's astonishment when, before his own eyes, his intended took his offering and hurled it down the stairs.

During one of the Linz Fairs, Bruckner and Waldeck strolled together along the Landstrasse, through Konrad-Voglstrasse to the exhibition in the market-place. They both bought their tickets and were just about to go in when a strikingly beautiful girl emerged from the exit. In an instant, Bruckner seized Waldeck by the arm and pointed her out to him. Waldeck now had to go back with Bruckner all the way along the Landstrasse, as far as the Franz-Josef-Platz, in pursuit of the unknown beauty. The lady vanished into the Hotel Zaininger (now Wolfinger). Bruckner gave the porter a tip and asked him to find out her name and background. She turned out to be a notary's daughter from Salzburg.

One morning Bruckner and Waldeck were walking in the Linz Hauptplatz. Ladies and servants were making their purchases at the vegetable market. Suddenly Bruckner grabbed Waldeck by the arm, pointed to a pretty kitchen-maid and said, 'Now Waldeck, there's a smart little wench!' Bruckner hurried off after her, dragging Waldeck with him. But as Bruckner hunted her and finally accosted her in the midst of stallkeepers and shoppers, Waldeck gave him the slip. A porter was despatched to enquire at the house where the lovely apparition was staying.

In later years, another Linz girl threw him into confusion. With instant resolve, he went boldly along the street to the object of his desire and said, 'I am Doctor Bruckner, will you allow me to pay you a visit?' Another example of how a woman could momentarily take possession of his heart. But it would also be possible to give examples of how Bruckner's simple, somewhat peasant-like appearance had its own peculiar appeal, so much so that many of his girl pupils felt more for him than mere puppy-love.

[Gräflinger, 109–10]

FRIEDRICH KLOSE

True to form, Friedrich Klose now gives a lovingly detailed account of one of Bruckner's 'little romantic episodes'. In the first paragraph Klose refers to a form of 'mental abnormality' that he had observed in the composer at Bayreuth; he does not go into detail, but some later (uncredited) anecdotes mention another form of the counting mania described by Karl Waldeck, and there are further hints in the section on Bruckner and Wagner, 'The Master of all Masters'.

One day he instructed me to call and collect him in the evening; the idea was for us to visit the trade exhibition in the Prater together. I arrived at his apartment at exactly the appointed time, and it was instantly clear that he was in good spirits. 'Perhaps – ' he said as we sauntered down the stairs – 'perhaps we'll have an adventure today.' What this might mean was a complete mystery to me, as indeed was Bruckner's whole behaviour. The show was in the Rotunda, a survival from the 1873 World Exhibition; this was a colossal domed structure, visible far and wide, a hundred metres in diameter, its coffered ceiling reaching as high as a church tower – an architectural wonder, it was said. Naturally I thought that we would begin our tour of the exhibits at the entrance – but I was wrong. Bruckner made straight for the middle, where stood one of the products of the Schlögel Paper Mill, an enormous coloured column surrounded by chairs. A series of walkways radiated out from this to the periphery, between which stood the great glass cases which held the exhibits. At first I thought that Bruckner meant to rest for a while, but no, far from it; instead of sitting down, he went constantly round and round the column, glancing along the gangways. This behaviour was so extraordinary that I began to fear a repetition of that mental abnormality that I had observed in the Master at our Bayreuth meeting in 1882. Suddenly he stood still, his eye fixed on three female figures looking closely at a glass case not far from us. Did Bruckner think that there was something worth seeing there? I had to presume so, for now he hurried into the next passageway and stared more through the glass casing than into it, devouring the group opposite with his eyes while they continued staring intently at the contents. Undoubtably it was these persons that interested Bruckner, so I began to take a closer look at them. They consisted of a respectable woman and two girls, apparently her daughters, one about seventeen, the other fourteen. And now everything was clear: the elder of the two had caught the Master's eye. She was actually more a child than a young woman, dressed simply but neatly. Yet there was nothing in her nice, innocent, but rather ordinary features that might explain Bruckner's passionate interest, unless it was that her enchanting, unspoilt quality spoke to something in his own childlike nature.

As the three women moved on to the next case, Bruckner did the same, once again squinting at the girl from the other side, a manoeuvre that was repeated as often as the women changed place. Aware of the absurdity of this behaviour, I tried to get Bruckner to go and look at some other exhibits. In vain. 'Come on. Come and have a look,' he urged impatiently and carried on flirting through the glass, while the girl shyly avoided his gaze.

Suddenly, up came Franz Weber, timpanist at the Hofoper, much valued by Hans Richter, and the charming young singer Ellen Forster, and their enthusiastic greeting of the Master brought this madness to a quick end. One could see how badly Bruckner took this interruption. But when Miss Forster put her hand on his shoulder in that uninhibited way all high-spirited actresses have, and asked 'When are we going to sing something of yours again, Herr Professor?' that was the end. Irritated even more by her discourteous, free manner, he snarled, 'How should I know?' and the astonished young woman turned quickly to me, leaving it to her companion to talk to the graceless gentleman. After we had said our goodbyes, the pleasure I felt in having got to know this much-admired singer personally inspired me to make a rather wicked comparison between Bruckner's penchant for the unremarkable Bürger's daughter and my altogether better taste in women. 'Now then, Herr Professor,' I said, 'Miss Forster is more to my taste', to which the Master quickly retorted, 'Well, go on then, if you're so hungry for French cooking.'

Meanwhile mother and daughters had vanished. Bruckner had realized, however, that the quickest way to find them again was to go back to the middle of the Rotunda, so he hurried to the paper column, walked around it again, and stared along the walkways. Suddenly his face lit up with fresh excitement: he had found her. She came over and sat down on one of the chairs at the base of the column. Immediately Bruckner did the same, taking care, however, to leave a space free between him and his intended, at the same time indicating to me, his face shining with joy, that I should sit down on his other side. And now a delightful scene began. Bruckner wanted to attract the girl's attention without giving his intentions away, so he directed his every utterance so that it could be heard just as well by his young neighbour on the left as it was by me on the right; in other words, he spoke looking straight ahead, every now and then stealing a glance at the girl to see if there was any sign of a reaction. 'The exhibition's quite a success,' he began. (Inquiring glance to the left – the girl stares into space; I, aware of my insignificance, silent – pause.) 'The electric lighting works very well.' (More enquiring glances left – the girl looks straight ahead; I keep quiet – pause.) 'It must have cost a fair bit to put this lot up.' (With mounting expectation, eyes left – the girl still stares in front, I stay silent – pause.) Now Bruckner could not control himself any longer. 'Miss,' – he turned to the unresponsive figure – 'Miss, I'm sure I've seen you somewhere before – could it have been at a Philharmonic concert?' Back comes the reply: she has never been to a Philharmonic concert. 'Then you look very like someone I did meet there.' With that they were off. And now, while mother and younger daughter sit silently on one side, and I on the other, the couple between us perform an exquisite duet, building to a climactic *stretta* when Bruckner asks if the girl comes to the exhibition often? 'Almost every day,' comes the answer. 'Ah, and may I ask your name?' her besotted examiner enquires eagerly. Like an obedient schoolgirl, she obeys. Hardly has Bruckner heard it than to my complete astonishment he springs up and heads straight for the exit. I follow, desperate to find out what this sudden flight means. 'Now we're off to the tavern,' declares Bruckner. 'Let's get Lehmann (the Vienna address-book) and find out where she lives.' No sooner said than done! But in the event it wasn't so simple; the surname in question filled whole columns of that immense book. But Bruckner would not be put off; like a sharp-minded criminologist he reached a conclusion: 'She told me she comes almost every day to the exhibition, so she can't live that far away.' So now all the bearers of that name who lived near the Prater were picked out, especially those whose circumstances matched the appearance of the women most closely. As I remember, it was a minor official in the Kaiser-Josephstrasse whom Bruckner selected as her father.

The next time I came for my lesson, I found Bruckner despondent. It was all over with the girl. Frau Kathi had been sent to enquire about her, and had found out from the caretaker that the girl was already engaged. Now I do not wish to speak ill of anyone, least of all the excellent Frau Kathi – on the contrary, it says a lot for her intelligence if she pocketed the money that Bruckner gave her for the tram, did not make the trip to the Kaiser-Josephstrasse and invented the story about the girl's betrothal.

Make of it what you will, the disappointed composer considered the whole business over and done with, only adding, with a resigned sigh, 'I am the unluckiest of lovers.'

[Klose, 117–22]

F. FORSTER

Councillor F[?] Forster of Linz provided this strange, sad little reminiscence for the massive Göllerich/Auer study, *Anton Bruckner – Ein Lebens- und Schaffenbild* ('Anton Bruckner – Life and Works'). Karl Aigner, who presumably related the story to Forster, was an official at the bank in St Florian, who also worked as organist and taught the choristers in the monastery. He helped prepare copies of some of Bruckner's works for publication, notably the Eighth Symphony. The events take place during one of Bruckner's summer visits to St Florian. The year is 1892: in other words, Bruckner was nearly sixty-eight.

Bruckner usually took his walks in the company of the music teacher Karl Aigner in the market or around St Florian. On one of these walks, the Master noticed a pretty girl of about sixteen, who greatly attracted his attention. She disappeared into a court building, which Bruckner then proceeded to walk past several times with Aigner. After a while, the beautiful young girl, Anna R., the daughter of the gaoler, appeared in the garden in front of the building. The Master suddenly stepped out in front of her, introduced himself and spoke to her affectionately. The lady, who now carries the name of Frau A. H., can still remember how at that first meeting, as on later occasions, he spoke with enthusiasm about his Ninth Symphony. 'Come, sit down (on the garden bench), and I'll tell you about the Ninth,' he used to say when he visited her with Aigner or his brother Ignaz. The parents did not stop the Master, who was admired everywhere, as his peculiarities in this respect were nothing new in St Florian. On one occasion the Master noticed some beautiful roses in the garden. He asked Anna if he was allowed to pick one, upon which he handed it, beaming, to his beloved.

On one occasion the time for the evening meal at the monastery (seven o'clock) arrived. Aigner pointed this out to the Master, but he was unable to leave Anna, and on being informed for the second time that it was time for dinner, he claimed not to be hungry. He did not appear at the table that evening. As one would expect, he was teased about his new conquest at the monastery, which annoyed him. 'The people of St Florian don't understand me,' he told Anna. 'I'm going back to Steyr.'

His 'dear child' looked particularly charming in the blue dress she had been wearing when Bruckner saw her for the first time. One day he asked her to put on the 'little blue dress' once again. The wish was fulfilled, and as Anna appeared in the requested blue dress, Bruckner was beside himself with delight. He tugged at the sleeves and said, 'Child, how sweet you look in that; my mother had clothes made of material just like that.' The Master's thoughts had rushed far back to the days of his youth, to – mother! As indeed Parsifal said in the flower garden – 'I had a mother!'

Jokingly, with an allusion to his always very short-cropped and now thinning hair, he once said, 'I could give you anything but a lock of my hair (women only ever want locks of hair from artists); otherwise I'd soon have no hair left.'

Shortly afterwards Anna went to Amstetten as a chambermaid to the then chief local government officer, Baron Lederer. Bruckner insisted on visiting the girl there on his return journey from Vienna, even though he did not know Baron Lederer. On 1 October he wrote to Anna from the parish presbytery in Steyr, 'My dear Fraülein, please find enclosed my photograph as promised. I would be grateful if you could send me yours. On Wednesday, 5 October, between two and three o'clock, I will be arriving in Amstetten by the midday train. Should I visit you now, or not until some time later? Please write and tell me. I kiss your hand. Yours, Bruckner.' Written on the back of the photograph, from the studio of A. Huber, Vienna 1, Goldschmiedgasse 4, is the dedication, 'To dear Frl. Anna R. . . . in deepest adoration. Dr A. Bruckner.'

The visit to Amstetten did actually take place. Bruckner was received in the Baron's drawing room, where he met Anna R. and stayed until the next train, to which Anna was allowed to accompany him. Later he sent her his visiting card with his address in Vienna so that she could visit him there. He explained that his housekeeper would meet her at the station and that he wanted to show her the sights of Vienna. Despite a further letter from the Master (which unfortunately went missing), the visit never took place.

The young girl did not reply, and so this strange episode came to an end.

[Göllerich/Auer, 2/1, 313–14]

Of course 'Bruckner and Women' should not be taken only to mean sexual (or not-quite-sexual) relationships. Women played important parts in Bruckner's life in other ways. In the last extract, Councillor Forster mentioned the composer's mother; according to Carl Hruby (p. 59), she remained 'the one true love' of Bruckner's life. Then there was his sister Nani, who looked after him from 1866, moving with him to Vienna two years later; her early death in 1870 was a severe blow. Soon afterwards, Bruckner took a housekeeper, Katharina ('Kathi') Kachelmayr, or Kachelmaier. Friedrich Klose has portrayed her as a benevolent, motherly influence, which the next extract tends to confirm, though it shows that their relationship could also be stormy.

AUGUST GÖLLERICH/MAX AUER

August Göllerich (1859–1923) was pupil and friend of Bruckner. He collected an enormous amount of material on the composer for his projected four-part study *Anton Bruckner – Ein Lebens- und Schaffenbild*, but lived to finish only the first volume. After his death, the work was completed by Max Auer (1880–1962). The following portrait of Frau Kathi seems to derive from Göllerich's own experience: he and Auer are on the whole scrupulous about acknowledging other sources.

Kathi Kachelmayr was a labourer's wife who looked after the housework for the Master faithfully and devotedly for twenty-six years until his death. For a wage of five guilders a month,* she went to Bruckner's house at particular times during the day, to tidy up and sometimes to prepare a meal for him. Frau Kathi had to be there at seven o'clock in the morning. The first thing to be seen to was the coffee, which she, as 'the eminent coffee-maker', prepared. Bruckner drank a good deal of coffee, though he took it very weak. With it, he would have a two-Kreutzer loaf of bread, of which he only ever ate the two ends. The dough in the middle was put on one side; Frau Kathi had to save it for the following day, when Bruckner would eat it at eleven o'clock for a midday meal with a small piece of meat brought from the inn the evening before. This was his routine, day in, day out.

Frau Kathi was never allowed to bring his coffee to him in his room. It remained on the stove until Bruckner, already dressed, came out. This was because she was not allowed to see him in his night-shirt. While he ate breakfast, Kathi had to sit down at the table with him and tell him something. If she had nothing to say he would chase her out, as she herself recalls. His relationship with her was one of utmost respect. If he had something 'delicate' to tell her he would say, 'Kathi, allow me to tell you, after all you're a woman.' He would probably be looking for advice and understanding in his many affairs of the heart. 'Just once in my life,

*According to Bruckner's pocket diaries, he paid her seven guilders a month from 1876 until his death.

when I was young, I kissed a girl,' he confessed to her in later years. He deeply regretted this, considering it a sin.

Directly after breakfast he would compose, and Kathi was no longer allowed in.

Just as in Beethoven's domestic life, Bruckner's impulsive nature often led to heated scenes with Frau Kathi; she would then simply not turn up the next day, and there remained nothing for Bruckner to do but to go and fetch her. At the start he often chased her out himself. Once, he even considered throwing her out of the window – as Handel did with the Italian prima donna – because he found a needle in his night-shirt, which Kathi had forgotten when she was darning. He claimed she wanted to stab him. He was already locking the door when Kathi yelled, 'Now you'll be shut in!' At this he returned to his senses, begged her forgiveness and let her cook a good supper in reconciliation. Often, when she had had enough of his overexcited behaviour, she would run away; then he would go to her house and bring her back. When he was in a good mood, especially in his later years, he would address her with the familiar 'du'.

There were also times, particularly when he was in the thick of composing, when he would let Frau Kathi prepare all his meals for him.

On Tuesdays, Fridays and Saturdays, he had to be at the Conservatory for eleven o'clock, though he never left before eleven. He went there in a one-horse carriage, so that he arrived just before quarter past.* In later years he often reported sick. Kathi then had to go and inform the usher, Binder (on the ground floor next to the porter's lodge).

On the other days of the week Bruckner gave private lessons or composed until two or three o'clock, while Frau Kathi cooked lunch. Kathi liked to make dumplings and sauerkraut with salted meat from St Florian or Vöcklabruck, which he particularly loved. On Fridays there was cream strudel, fried noodles and also what he used to call 'chocolate soup'. On rarer occasions there was *Einbrennsuppe*, often steamed noodles and milk, which he used to call 'rainworms', and 'Kirschenschober', Kathi's own version of *Heuschober*, which was a type of round sponge cake with cherries.

*Apparently it was accepted practice at this time for lectures to begin at quarter past the hour.

1 Bruckner c. 1854.

2 Bruckner at the organ. Silhouette by Otto Böhler. 3 Bruckner during his Linz years. 4 Wagner offering snuff to Bruckner. Silhouette by Otto Böhler. 5 Wagner welcoming Bruckner to Bayreuth. Silhouette by Otto Böhler.

6 Simon Sechter (1788–1867), Bruckner's teacher. 7 Max von Oberleithner. 8 Ferdinand Löwe, Bruckner's pupil and later friend.

9 Friedrich Eckstein ('Samiel'). 10 Karl Waldeck.
11 Franz Schalk 12 Josef Schalk.

13 The Red Hedgehog Restaurant, site of the alleged meetings between Bruckner and Brahms. 14 Bruckner's brother, Ignaz. 15 Bruckner c. 1890.

16 Bruckner at his Bösendorfer. c. 1894. OPPOSITE: 17 Bruckner asleep, shortly before his death. 18 One of the last photographs of Bruckner, showing from l. to r. Dr Heller, Frau Kathi, Anton Bruckner, his brother Ignaz and Dr Schrötter. In modern copies of this photograph Dr Heller has, mysteriously, been removed. 19 Bruckner's death mask.

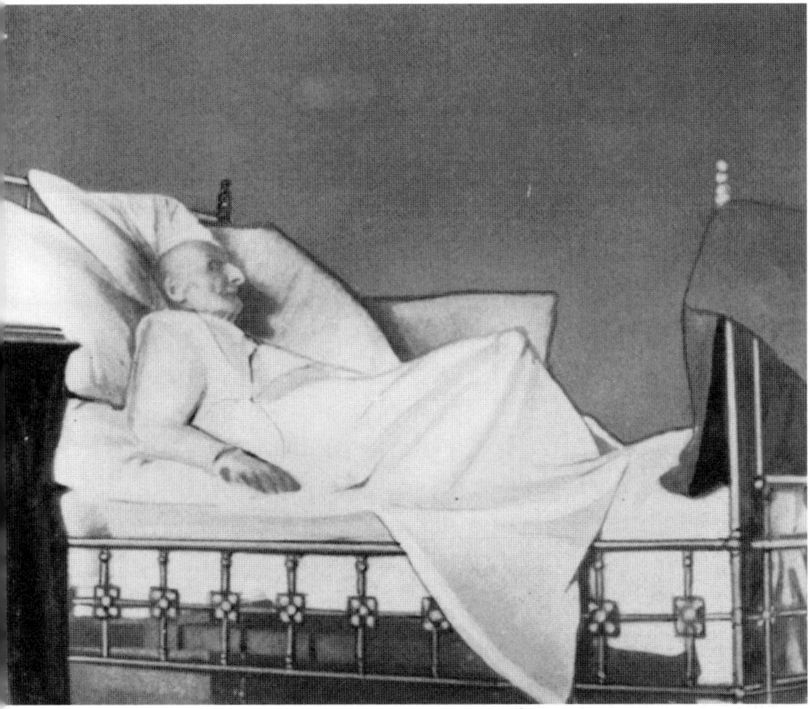

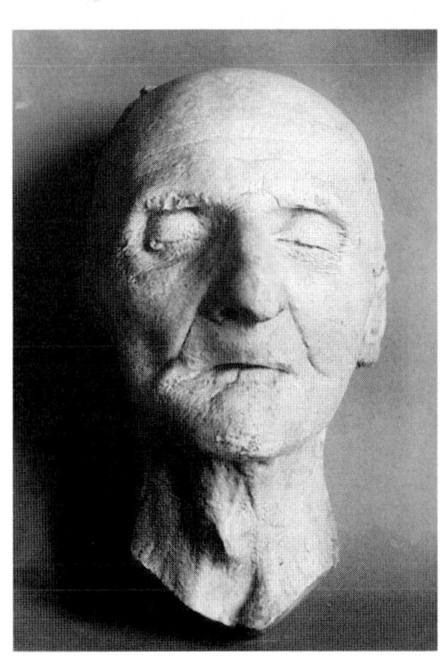

20 Bruckner's memorial tablet, St. Florian.

On days when he was not teaching, he absorbed himself so much in his work that he never noticed the meal Kathi prepared for him; often he did not eat until eleven o'clock at night, when he usually went to the 'Kugel' inn for a meal with beer. With his huge appetite, he would then catch up on his lunch and his evening meal by ordering three portions of noodle soup and equally large quantities of meat dishes.

[Göllerich/Auer, 4/1, 121–4]

CARL HRUBY

Carl Hruby tells another Bruckner love-story. Again, the events take place during one of Bruckner's Upper Austrian summer holidays. Note that, like Forster in the previous narrative, Hruby draws attention to Bruckner's feelings for his mother, 'the one true love of his life', which may throw light on his life-long inability to form mature sexual relationships with women. The 'friend Grossauer' Hruby refers to is the Upper Austrian musician Ludwig Grossauer. As for the girl, Hruby later gives her name as 'Fräulein Betty R'.

There are many false notions about Bruckner's relations with women, and about the role love, that powerful motivator of great artists, played in his life. Actually Bruckner never knew true 'love', a really great passion for a similarly high-minded woman – just like his artistic antithesis Johannes Brahms. With women, he was as shy and naïve as a ten-year-old schoolboy. The explanation can be found if one looks thoroughly at his life history. Sorrow and care were his inseparable companions from earliest youth to full manhood; and so he had little time or inclination to attempt to turn himself into a dashing gallant. 'Ten hours at the piano, three hours at the organ – that was my daily regime; any time left over was for – recovering,' he put it with grim irony.

As for 'casual' acquaintances, throughout his life he was protected from anything like that by the pure radiance of his natural chastity. The one true love of his life, according to his own words, was his revered mother, of whom he had Zinnegar draw a portrait on her deathbed. Only once did it seem that Lady Love [*Frau Minne*] might have worked her way deeper into his heart, and that the peace and mental balance of the old man might be seriously endangered. I know enough to be able to tell the following story. In 1885, as was his habit, Bruckner spent his summer holiday at the presbytery in Steyr, where he was a very welcome guest. One day he went to a garden party with his oft-mentioned friend Grossauer. While some music was being played he suddenly saw a very young, indescribably charming girl, the daughter of a respectable couple from Linz, sitting at a nearby table. In his typically impetuous manner he insisted that Grossauer introduce him to the girl's family, with whom Grossauer had a nodding acquaintance. But Grossauer was not quick enough off the mark, and so Bruckner – after informing Grossauer that he was an 'arsehole' – decided to do the honours himself, in his own inimitable way.

He went quickly over to the table where the lovely girl sat, in the process knocking over a chair. The apology necessitated by this gave him the opportunity to introduce himself. And now Bruckner appeared completely transformed! He danced waltzes and *Ländler* with his beloved for half the night, like a sturdy farmer's boy, and Grossauer sat transfixed with astonishment at the sight of the Master so light and graceful on his feet. The poor girl however hardly knew what to make of the compliments showered on her in the course of the evening by this famous man, known throughout Steyr, and old enough to be her grandfather. Some days later he invited everybody to the presbytery and played the Adagio from his Eighth Symphony to a rapt audience, the inspiration for which – he told me – had come over a glass of 'Pilsner'. According to Grossauer, he had never been known to play with such fervour before. How things developed after this I cannot say. Bruckner is even said to have proposed, but he never married. He may have come to the realization that at his age it would have been too great a risk to love any other bride than that consistently chaste beauty, his ever-faithful, compliant, lofty art.

[Hruby, 35–7]

Were there moments when the 'pure radiance' of Bruckner's 'natural chastity' failed to protect him? The next two stories, both from the same writer, give varied impressions: in the first, Bruckner is once again revealed as the child of nature, too pure even to recognize a compromising situation; the second suggests that he might not have been so innocent after all.

ALMA MAHLER

Erinnerungen und Briefe ('Memories and Letters') by Alma Mahler (*née* Schindler, 1879–1964) is a fund of anecdote, gossip and sharp personal insight, mostly concerning her husband, Gustav Mahler, but including many other Viennese luminaries. In the words of Hans Keller, 'there isn't a boring line in this racily written book'. Alma Mahler devotes several pages of her book to Bruckner stories, the majority, it seems, deriving from her husband, who had been a friend and supporter of the older composer during his student days and had helped prepare the four-hand piano arrangement of the Third Symphony.

Mahler had a young friend whom he admired devoutly. This was Hans Rott.* It was Rott's Symphony that failed to win the competition even though it was the finest entry. One hot summer day, Rott's mother knocked on Bruckner's door to find out how her son was progressing. The response was a loud 'Come in' and she entered the room. Bruckner advanced towards her stark naked, fresh from his bath-tub, to shake her by the hand. She fled, screaming. For a long time he was unable to understand this: 'What's wrong with the woman?' When engrossed in his work he was oblivious of everything else. On hot days he used to compose in the tub, with the score on a chair beside him.

Several versions of that story appeared in print after Bruckner's death, but Alma Mahler is the only one to name the unlucky woman. Unfortunately the identification is impossible: Hans Rott's mother died in 1860, eight years before Bruckner took up residence in Vienna,

*Hans Rott (1858–1884) was one of Bruckner's favourite pupils, the composer of an impressive Symphony in E major (1880). He died, in a lunatic asylum, at the age of twenty-five.

when Rott himself would have been barely two years old.

In the next story Alma Mahler does specify her source: the German choral conductor Siegfried Ochs (1858–1929), who gave the 1891 Berlin première of Bruckner's *Te Deum* and became friendly with the composer. The 'Bruckner Mass' Alma Mahler refers to is almost certainly the *Te Deum*, as the mention of a 'festival' and 'a big party in Bruckner's honour' tend to confirm – in which case the contrast between this and Max von Oberleithner's version of the Berlin trip (below) is all the more striking.

Siegfried Ochs told me a touching Bruckner story, in which he himself had played a part. Ochs conducted a Bruckner Mass at a festival in Berlin. Afterwards he had arranged a big party in Bruckner's honour. Bruckner telephoned that afternoon to say that he could come only if he could bring his fiancée. Fiancée? Since when had he been engaged? With a sense of foreboding, Ochs rushed off to the hotel. He found Bruckner in a state of utter dejection. The chambermaid had suddenly appeared the night before and . . . in short, when the morning came she had burst into tears, saying that he had robbed her of her honour and would have to marry her. Bruckner had promised to do so, and now he was betrothed. Ochs summoned the girl and asked her directly how much she wanted. The sum was considerable. Bruckner overflowed with gratitude and kissed the protesting Ochs's hand.

[Alma Mahler: *Erinnerungen und Briefe*, 132–5]

MAX VON OBERLEITHNER

Now for a first-hand account of the Berlin trip. Max von Oberleithner accompanied Bruckner for most of his stay in Berlin, and on visits to other German cities. In Berlin he stayed in the same hotel as Bruckner, the Kaiserhof. Oberleithner also reports a Brucknerian romantic entanglement, but the outcome here is very different from that of Alma Mahler's story. Oberleithner's chapter (subtitled 'Bruckner and Women') is reproduced almost in its entirety; only two short para-

> graphs, reporting an anecdote about Beethoven, are omitted. Oberleithner draws a plausible connection between Bruckner's 'imposed restraint' and his neurotic disorders. This differs from Karl Waldeck's explanation (p. 46), though, like Waldeck, Oberleithner makes significant mention of the Kyrie from the F minor Mass in connection with Bruckner's mental collapse – the reference to Bad Kreuzen confirms that the date he means is 1867, not 1864. Later on, Oberleithner has a startling revelation concerning Bruckner's 'powerful masculine urges' . . .

In May 1891 Bruckner received an invitation from Professor Siegfried Ochs to the first performance of the *Te Deum* in Berlin, which was to take place in June in a Music Festival organized by Liszt's Allgemeine Deutsche Musikverein.

We arrived in Berlin a few days before the concert and put up in the Hotel 'Kaiserhof'. Next morning, Bruckner wanted to see the historic corner window on Unter den Linden in the Palace of the Crown Prince. It was then that I realized for the first time that Bruckner could not retain the appearance of a room in his memory, because he ran back several times and in the end he counted the windows, so as to keep the image in his mind.

His mind was set so exclusively on the working out of musical ideas that his visual memory failed him, a problem which grew daily, the longer the journey kept him from his musical work. At midday August Göllerich and Friedrich Rösch presented themselves and we went off to the Tiergarten to see the monument of Queen Louise and her consort. There Bruckner's nervous behaviour broke out again, creating a bad atmosphere because he heard Göllerich ask me if I had witnessed anything similar that morning. The choral rehearsal for the *Te Deum* that evening was a great relief; the choir was extraordinarily secure and well prepared. The explanation followed later – the Vienna Singverein was made up solely of amateurs, while the best part of the Berlin Philharmonic Chorus comprised professional singers. Bruckner was particularly impressed by the sopranos' security in the highest registers. The next day we visited Hofkapellmeister Sucher. From the manner in which Sucher spoke to Bruckner, you would have thought they were close friends, although Sucher has never actually done anything for his friend. Bruckner made frequent visits to the Catholic church where he prayed constantly.

The performance of the *Te Deum* came at the end of an overly long concert. The programme started at eight o'clock, the *Te Deum* did not begin until eleven. Even so it was huge success. Again and again Bruckner had to make his grateful bows. Siegfried Ochs directed the choir and soloists excellently, though the orchestra sounded less good. Anyway, he had done all he could to give the Master a worthy reception and, wonder of wonders, the Berlin press wrote quite favourably about the work, and not one single review was as malicious or withering as the majority (alas!) in Vienna.

So, as far as artistic matters were concerned, the stay in Berlin went off well. Unfortunately it also allowed one of Bruckner's weaknesses to lead to a misunderstanding – one that may have future repercussions.

The first day after our arrival in Berlin Bruckner called me to his room in the Kaiserhof and introduced me to the chambermaid, Ida, a young girl with pleasant manners. Bruckner still toyed constantly with the idea of getting married, and every now and then he would ask me whether I liked a certain girl and whether I thought she would make a good wife for him. So I did not think it unusual that he should ask me the same question about Ida. Unfortunately I could not summon up much enthusiasm for Ida, and this was probably the reason why he never took me into his confidence again, for he often wrote to her. I heard later that she replied to his letters, legitimately or not, as his fiancée.

It is however quite certain that Bruckner did not have intimate relations with her, nor did he marry her nor anyone else, though only recently the newspapers did represent the event in such terms, as though the 'pure fool' had fallen from grace in the Kaiserhof.

'Bruckner and Women' truly deserves a chapter in its own right. As a child he was inspired to become a composer by hearing Schubert *Lieder* sung at St Florian. When one of Bruckner's religious teachers (a man he strongly admired) learned of this, he told him that if he wanted to realize his ambition he should keep himself apart from women (Bruckner told me this himself, and the fact that he quoted it in his old age proves its genuineness). During his time as an assistant teacher, Bruckner fell in love with a girl, and she looked on him with favour; but they did not have the means to get married. The thought of this made him melancholy, and he regretted the loss of what should have been a great happiness (though it would probably have turned out to be a misfortune).

In the years that followed he was so overwhelmed with work, especially as organist at St Florian, that he could not even think of marriage. He did indeed admire many beauties in Linz, but in so doing he experienced many rejections, particularly as it was always the youngest girls that inflamed his ardour, and he was the clumsiest of men when it came to winning a woman's heart; nor was he particularly wealthy.

When the girls made fun of him, he would give vent to his anger by calling them 'Salsen', an Upper Austrian expression meaning something like 'trollops'. He was always ripe for infatuation, and his emotions caught fire very quickly – if not, he would hardly have been a musician. Certainly he was no woman-hater – quite the opposite: many melodic passages in his symphonies owe their inspiration to some pretty face that took his fancy. But nothing further came of these longings. He never tried to be captivating or seductive with women; in short, he was the opposite of Don Juan. What he always wanted was to be married, and as a strict Catholic he knew this would mean for life.

It was a happy fate that protected him from marriage, though while he was in Linz the conflict between powerful masculine urges and imposed restraints brought about a mental crisis, manifest in overwork and hypernervousness, so that in 1864 [*sic*] he had to go to Bad Kreuzen for the cold-water cure. But even there he found no peace. He counted the flowers on the women's summer dresses (the same mania for counting that I had noticed during our visit to the historic window in Berlin); in a word, it was a fierce struggle between his longing for a woman and his decision to devote himself exclusively to composition. Bruckner told how he had been afraid he might go under in this struggle; for that reason, the Kyrie of the F minor Mass was begun in a mood of deepest sorrow, and it was only by dedicating himself to musical work that he was delivered from the threat of madness. It was not Bad Kreuzen that cured him, but the very thing the doctors had forbidden him: the resumption of his work. In this crisis, one reads the true signs of a struggling artistic soul.

It is likely that Bruckner still contemplated marriage later in Vienna, and perhaps he got as far as a proposal; but one can be sure that the difference in age and ideas between a great symphonist and a young girl became even greater. Sometimes he was able to assess the situation with humour, as the following remark shows. Frau Schwarz told me that when she was a student at the women's teacher-training college, Bruckner (who taught music there) appeared at the first lesson and, catching sight of the flock of young women, said: 'Till today I've stayed a bachelor, but perhaps that'll change now.'

Once, during my time with him (that is, 1890–92), he told me, 'Yesterday I saw a real beauty. We'll go to the same place today at the same time (about eight o'clock in the evening) and perhaps she'll turn up again.' He was not quite sure whether one of the girls who went by was his Ideal or not, so he sent me to ask her if she had passed the same way the day before. Naturally I did no such thing, but came back with the news that he had been mistaken. After spending an hour in the deepest agitation, he suddenly pulled himself together and set off with me to the Gasthaus, where he drowned his sorrows in Pilsner beer . . .

Some years after the first performance of the Seventh Symphony under Nikisch in Leipzig, Bruckner remarked that 'The most beautiful woman I've ever seen is the actress Salbach.' On our return journey from Berlin we stopped in Dresden in order to see her. We called at her house but she was not at home. So that evening we waited by the stage door of the theatre where she was appearing. The caretaker announced her as she got out of her carriage, otherwise Bruckner would probably have disgraced himself because he was never very good at recognizing women he had seen. She was a slender, imposing apparition – Homer would have called her a high-bosomed woman – who responded very amiably to the old man as he removed his soft, wide-brimmed hat and bowed deferentially.

Then we took our places in the theatre. *Die Welt, in der man langweilt* was playing, and every time one of the actresses came on stage Bruckner nudged me and asked. 'Is that her?' (He meant, is that Fräulein Salbach?) Always I had to answer 'No'; but when the English governess with the pince-nez and the comic blond wig made her entrance, and I was at last able to whisper, 'Here she is', he was convinced I was trying to fool him. That was the end of all his enthusiasm, as her appearance in this role naturally gave little delight to the eye; and so we set off after the first act for a Pilsner beer. Bruckner obviously had no idea what Fräulein Salbach looked like, even when he enthused about how beautiful she was, though at that time in Leipzig I cannot deny that he was right.

At this point I should mention a peculiar experience during our time in Berlin. I had to help Bruckner pack so that we could get to the station on time. Amongst his effects was a huge pair of swimming-trunks. In answer to my enquiring glance he explained, 'You see, I suffer from wet dreams, and I put these on at night so that no one will find anything on the bed-linen.' – And this was a man of sixty-seven! This was during the time of Ida. If anything had really happened between them, surely the swimming-trunks would not have been needed.

Bruckner's chastity was acknowledged by all of us. It was said that Adalbert Goldschmidt and Mottl engaged the services of a *demi-mondaine* and told Bruckner that she was a Russian princess, whose patronage was worth having, and who wanted to meet him. Bruckner went to her and she carried out those two young reprobates' plan of attack with some enthusiasm. Bruckner ran from her like the chaste Joseph from Potiphar's wife. I think these observations are enough to show that the Ida episode was quite meaningless. It would not have lasted so long if Ida had lived in Vienna; one can hold on to a dream longer in letters.

In Dresden, Bruckner called on Herr von Schuch; he was very kind to us and arranged tickets for us for productions of *Rheingold* and *Walküre* on 5 and 6 June. Otherwise Schuch never did much for Bruckner. Amongst the conductors in the larger German cities at that time the majority came from Austria: Schuch, Sucher, Mottl, Weingartner; but none of these would declare themselves for Bruckner. Mottl made up for this later on, but only Nikisch and Levi in Munich were true pioneers for Bruckner. Nikisch was of Slavic blood, Levi Jewish – remarkable that these should have been the first great conductors to appreciate the greatness of the 'Deutsche Michel'. The Catholic, German Austrians, who should have understood him more easily, remained behind.

Otherwise, our stay in Dresden was quite unpleasant. When Bruckner had got over his joy at the success of the performance of the *Te Deum*, his nervous mania returned. In the Catholic church, where he prayed often and long, he heard that the king's coffin lay in the crypt below. Visits to the crypt were not permitted, so for hour after hour Bruckner tried to peer inside through the cellar-like windows in the street, hoping to catch a glimpse of a coffin, and summoning me as a witness. I tried injecting a little humour into the situation by mimicking the Saxon dialect – something I am rather good at. At first, Bruckner was fascinated by my efforts, but it was impossible to get him away from the church, and in the end there was nothing left for me but to announce that I was going back to the Hotel Bellevue to pack and be ready to go at eleven o'clock, as I had to return to Vienna. A quarter of an hour later Bruckner appeared in the hotel and we drove to the station. On the way he suddenly asked me how tall the houses were around here. I answered, 'Most of them are only two storeys high, but some have three or four.' 'I haven't seen any with three storeys,' he said and promptly insisted that the carriage turn back – we were just coming up to the station – so that we could find a higher building. (Today the houses around the station are taller.) I declared that I would come with him, but for no longer than our departure time would allow, otherwise I would get out and go to Vienna alone. Luckily we soon discovered a three- or four-storeyed house. Bruckner counted the storeys several times, and then we set off for the station.

Having got there, we installed ourselves in the restaurant car. Bruckner ordered beer and suddenly he was his old, amiable self again, completely free of nervous symptoms. As soon as he got back to his work in Vienna, the whole dreadful episode was forgotten, and shortly afterwards he set off to Steyr for his customary summer holiday.

[Oberleithner, 55–66]

III

THE MUSICIAN

Divine Fantasies

Some portraits of Bruckner are clearly intended to increase our sense of wonder: how could such a 'simple' soul have produced such extraordinary music? Others, like Max von Oberleithner, suggest deeper connections between the man and the work: instances where Bruckner's behaviour or revealed state of mind throws light on the musical content or on the process of composition. We now move closer to the work-desk – and to the organ console: Bruckner may be remembered today as a composer, but, as Friedrich Eckstein indicated, for much of his life he was more widely appreciated as an organist. His recitals in Nancy and Paris (1869) and in London (1871) brought him moments of rare personal triumph: in Sepp Stöger's reminiscence, Bruckner contrasted them bitterly with his experiences in Vienna. As we shall see, the task of perfecting musical ideas on paper was to become increasingly arduous for Bruckner, especially as his notorious 'revision mania' intensified; in contrast, the organ-loft held the possibility of a more spontaneous and purely enjoyable kind of artistic experience.

THE MORNING ADVERTISER

The following anonymous review appeared in a London newspaper, *The Morning Advertiser*, on Friday, 1 September 1871, a few days after Bruckner's recital on the Albert Hall's new Willis organ. Accounts of his success there vary. The critic of the *Musical Standard* (12 August 1871) makes a point of preferring the English organist William Thomas Best to any of his 'continental rivals', and traditional English xenophobia clearly influenced one or two other journalistic commentators. But on the whole, the reception seems to have been very enthusiastic. As a result of his Albert Hall appearance, Bruckner was invited to give a further five concerts at the Crystal Palace, and there was talk of inviting him back for a tour of England the following year. Bruckner is said to have remarked, 'In England my music is really understood' – ironic, given the patronizing indifference of most English musicians and critics to his major works in later years.

PROFESSOR BRUCKNER FROM VIENNA

When the International Exhibition and Royal Albert Hall were opened, the Council issued an invitation to artists of all nations to come over and test the excellence of the great organ. Amongst those who accepted this invitation was Herr Anton Bruckner, Court Organist and professor at the Conservatoire of Vienna. The executions by this disciple of art are truly excellent, and quite worthy of the Fatherland of Haydn and Mozart. Herr Bruckner executes the classical compositions of Bach, Mendelssohn and others with a facility which leaves the hearer nothing to desire, and which would certainly even satisfy the composers themselves in the highest degree. But where Herr Bruckner excels is in his improvisations, where you find a great easiness and abundance of ideas, and the ingenious method by which such an idea is carried out – grave or solemn, melodious or charming, brilliant or grand – is very remarkable. The London public has fully acknowledged Herr Bruckner's perfect execution, and many have expressed a hope that this first visit may not be the last. We join in this wish, and indeed add another, namely that Herr Bruckner may publish some of his most successful compositions for the benefit and enjoyment of the musical public, who, we are sure, would be very pleased to become better acquainted with the works of this thorough artist.

[*The Morning Advertiser*, Friday, 1 September 1871]

The unnamed reviewer in *The Morning Advertiser* reserves his highest praise for Bruckner's improvisations. With few exceptions, descriptions of Bruckner the organist concentrate on this aspect of his playing. Carl Hruby summarizes Bruckner's own account of his examination at the Piaristenkirche, Vienna, in November 1861. The object of this examination was to demonstrate a level of academic competence sufficient to qualify the entrant as a 'Teacher of Harmony and Counterpoint at Conservatoria'. Evidently Bruckner rose above and beyond the demands of the occasion.

CARL HRUBY

He often told us, in wickedly ironic terms, about his so-called 'examination', in which he was called upon to give proof of his 'theoretical capability'. It took place in the Piaristenkirche. Professor Sechter wrote out a four-bar theme which – after Dessoff* had refused to do it – Herbeck** extended to eight bars. The theme was given to Bruckner. He stared, undecided, at the paper for a long time, and the 'examination committee' began to grow suspicious. Then he sat calmly at the organ and worked the theme up into a tremendous fugue, which overflowed into an even longer free fantasy. The members of the committee broke up and went their separate ways. As Herbeck was leaving he was heard to say, 'He should have examined us.'

[Hruby, 40]

AUGUST STRADAL

The next account describes the style of Bruckner's playing in later life. Given that August Stradal was a pupil of Liszt, we may presume that he was not easily impressed by technical agility. Stradal also gives some idea of the kind of themes Bruckner borrowed for his improvisations – not the most obvious selection for performance in church, at least not in the late nineteenth century. In the light of what Carl Hruby says about Bruckner's feelings for his mother (pp. 59–60), the

*Otto Dessoff (1835–92): German conductor and composer, chief conductor of the Vienna Philharmonic concerts until 1875; his appreciation of Bruckner's improvisations did not extend to his written compositions.

**Johann Herbeck (1831–77), Austrian conductor and composer, conductor of the Musikverein Concerts and, from 1870, director of the Vienna Opera. He was one the composer's earliest supporters in the Austrian capital. It was Herbeck who arranged Bruckner's appointment at the Vienna Conservatory in 1868.

> choice of the 'wonderful and heartfelt theme' from Act I of *Siegfried* must be significant.

It is not easy to describe Bruckner's organ-playing in such a way as to help the reader to imagine it; indeed a true description is made particularly difficult by the fact that when I first became his private student Bruckner was almost sixty years old. As a result he occasionally made some minor technical errors, as his fingers already trembled a little from time to time. Above all I must stress that Bruckner's organ-playing was the expression of a true genius and possessed a monumental quality. There was no false sentimentality, no daintiness, no fancy touches played purely for special effect; all this was rendered unnecessary by the greatness with which he filled every piece. At the time when I heard Bruckner playing the organ he clearly felt that he had already conquered the instrument; his very existence was now dedicated to the composition of symphonies and church music. Bruckner played the organ purely to give pleasure to others. As I have mentioned, his fingers had lost some of their former technical skill; however, it was amazing to witness the tremendous agility of his feet as they moved over the pedals.

United in Bruckner's playing – in addition to the technical qualities he displayed, despite his age – was a high degree of perception, depth of expression, passion and songfulness.

Bruckner rarely played the work of Bach or other old Masters; he improvised mainly on ideas from Wagner or created a powerful fugue on the basis of any theme he chose.

Once in the votive chapel he improvised on a motif from the transformation music from *Parsifal*.

On another occasion I heard him playing on the great organ at Klosterneuberg, when he selected that wonderful and heartfelt theme from the first act of *Siegfried*, in which Siegfried thinks of his mother. He also improvised in the court chapel, where he had to accompany hymns on a Sunday afternoon. At such times, once the hymns were over, he would take one of their themes as a basis; once he chose a theme from Beethoven's C sharp minor quartet and composed a splendid fantasy which lasted almost half an hour. He also practised this art on the organ in his room at home.

[Göllerich/Auer, 4/2, 84–5]

KARL ALMEROTH

Karl Almeroth (1852–1906) was a Viennese manufacturer who became a friend of Bruckner and arranged much-needed financial support for him. He accompanied the composer on many of his trips, putting his carriage at Bruckner's disposal, for which Bruckner gave him the nickname 'Wagerl' (literally, 'little carriage' or 'wagon'). This tantalizing description of one of Bruckner's later organ 'fantasies' first appeared as a review in the Linz daily newspaper.

On 28 August 1885 Bruckner gave an organ concert in St Florian for his friends and admirers, to which hordes of music enthusiasts made their pilgrimage. On that day St Florian turned into Little Bayreuth. Bruckner's admirers arrived at the monastery by every possible form of transport – in carriages and carts, by rail and on foot – in order to hear the sublime songs which Bruckner was able to coax from the magnificent instrument. Shortly before half past three the monastery chapel filled up, and soon the friendly face of our dear Bruckner appeared at the organ. On the organ case was hung a giant laurel wreath, adorned with a gleaming ribbon in the town colours of Steyr, on which this great truth was written in golden letters: 'To the Master of German music'. (It had been paid for by two ladies from Steyr, Frau Meta Moritsch and Fräulein Gisela Schneider). The concert began at half past three and Bruckner gave an excellent example of one of his world-famous improvisations. Beginning quietly, continually swelling up until it reached unexpected power, the sounds of the magnificent lamentation on the death of Siegfried from *Götterdämmerung* shook the audience. Bruckner then brought all his genius to bear in a contrapuntal reworking of the piece; but Siegfried's lamentation was soon joined by a new and equally sublime, solemn dirge: it was Bruckner's own funeral music from the Adagio of his Seventh Symphony, which he wrote in deepest grief on the death of Wagner. Then the heavens cleared and a lofty intermezzo in the style of Handel sang out. This jubilant song which followed the funeral music was interwoven with a theme from the Eighth Symphony, which had been completed in Steyr. The

'Walsungen' and 'Siegfried' motifs from the *Ring* returned once again. This time, however, the grief had disappeared, and powerful singing lines resounded in all registers, rushing and rejoicing towards the end of the piece. Having just played what was perhaps one of his most magnificent fantasies, Bruckner sat by the organ like an emperor, in the full realization that he had created something outstanding. Bruckner's artistic achievement had stirred us and lifted our spirits powerfully, and it would be hard to express in mere words our thankfulness for what he gave us.

[Göllerich/Auer, 2/1, 292–4]

SIMON LEDERMULLER

Unfortunately verbal descriptions are almost all we have regarding Bruckner's organ improvisations; however, Fr Simon Ledermüller of St Florian includes a few brief musical examples in his letters to a fellow cleric and friend of Bruckner, Oddo (born Raphael) Loidol of Kremsmünster (to whom Bruckner dedicated his motets *Christus factus est* and *Locus iste*). At best, Ledermüller offers only skeletal impressions of the musical substance, but his second letter gives some hint of a musical argument. On these occasions Bruckner appears to have improvised on themes of his own invention.

St Florian, 4 April 1882

Professor Bruckner played magnificently. For the prelude on Easter Sunday he played, first of all, the theme:

He then developed this theme in increasingly fast figures until at the end it sounded like this:

If I am not mistaken, he introduced the pedal in the following way:

The postlude [Nachspiel] went something like this:

etc., then in D major, then in E major, etc.

In the afternoon during Vespers he began with the theme:

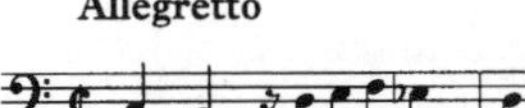

and finished with:

I'll tell you the rest when I see you.
Your friend,
Simon Ledermüller.

St Florian, 8 August 1882

Professor Bruckner is already at St Florian. He played the great organ at Herr Aichberger's first mass. Everything went beautifully. Professor Bruckner had some bad luck in Bayreuth – somebody stole over 300 guilders from him. Today, 8 August, there were several gentlemen at St Florian. On this occasion he gave another concert. It was organized in a similar way to the one held last year. The theme was the one he had worked on at Easter, but in greater detail. He also gave a concert a few days ago; I'll note down the theme which he developed. It required him to modulate continually, which meant that one's natural expectations were never fulfilled, with strangely fascinating results. It sounded like this:

Allegretto

The piece began in G minor. From this key he then moved through a number of other keys, as the theme demands. The concert was exceptionally fine. Bruckner sends you his best wishes. I had not been to see him until very recently, otherwise I would have written to you sooner. Next week he departs for Vienna, as it is his turn to play at the Court Chapel, then he is coming back for 28 August. Your friend,
Simon Ledermüller

[Göllerich/Auer, 2/1, 275–80 *passim*]

The striking image in Karl Almeroth's account was of Bruckner seated at the organ 'like an emperor', in full command of a great artistic event. The next account shows Bruckner on the receiving end of a kind of sublime practical joke, though the idea behind it appears to have been his own.

JULIA BAYER

A close friend of Bruckner, Julia Bayer (1862–1921) was the second wife of Franz Xaver Bayer, a choral conductor in Steyr, and the mother of Julius Bayer (see pp. 106–7). Bruckner regularly spent part of his summer holiday with them between the years 1888 and 1893. Here, Julia Bayer describes a performance of Bruckner's D minor Mass at Steyr in 1893, for which the composer played the organ. Franz Bayer's instruction to the bellows-operator to stop the air supply to the organ *specifically* at the solo in the Credo confirms the impression that Bruckner provided a continuo, though what kind of continuo that might have been (i.e. how much improvised decoration there was) is unfortunately not revealed. The narrative begins after a performance of Beethoven's Mass in C, conducted by Franz Bayer.

The high quality of the performance was confirmed by no less a person than Bruckner, who said to the choir leader: 'If you can perform the C major Mass like that, then you can do the same with my Mass in D minor at Easter!'

The Master's D minor Mass! Bayer took fright, for this was even harder than Beethoven's Mass in C major . . . The performance did indeed come to pass. One Easter Sunday the town's parish church was filled with a crowd of several thousand people, many of whom were in fact hoping that something dreadful might happen. Bayer had gathered together his most faithful choristers. Bruckner sat down at the organ and immediately brought the crowd under his control by giving the Mass a worthy introduction with one his magnificent preludes. The singers and musicians knew what was at stake. This knowledge, combined with the sight of the old Master at the organ, made them give the performance their all.

The Kyrie and the Gloria were performed without any cause for complaint. Despite the crowds of people, the church was filled with a solemn silence. The Credo began. The D minor Mass is an Easter Mass in the truest sense of the word; this Credo can be compared to no other, because it portrays the death and ascension of the Redeemer in such a masterful way. '*Et sepultus est*' – 'and he was buried.' A solo organ accompanies the body of Christ to the grave in indescribably moving tones . . .

Bayer had prepared a surprise for Bruckner at the aforementioned organ solo. On several occasions the Master had stated that the solo ought to be played from the high altar. Perhaps he hoped to achieve a special effect from the distance, or did he also picture the high altar as the grave of Christ? He never explained any further.

Now, because it was Holy Week a harmonium had been placed in the presbytery. Bayer had ordered that it be positioned behind the altar, together with a player who had been specially instructed as to what to do. The bellows-operator at the great organ had been told not to allow any air to pass through the instrument in this particular part of the Mass.

The moment arrived. The orchestra faded away and Bruckner pressed the keys, about to say his musical prayer to the Lord. But – what happened? The organ made no sound. But, as if from far way in the distance, the wonderful chords sounded from the high altar above in a gentle *piano*.

That was too much for the Master. For a moment his face seemed frozen, and then large tears began to roll down over his cheeks. His body trembled with emotion . . .

[Julia Bayer, 'Anton Bruckner in Steyr' reproduced in Grassberger and Partsch, *Bruckner – skizziert*, 66–7]

Bruckner does seem to have been rather less emperor-like when he conducted, even after long experience as a choral director. Linda Schönbeck (p. 20) recalled 'a funny scene or two' during some of Bruckner's rehearsals in Linz, but she had nothing but praise for the musical results. An unnamed member of the Vienna Philharmonic Orchestra, previously a chorister in the Vienna Boys' Choir, now recalls his youthful experience of Bruckner as conductor.

ANON

Bruckner certainly did not wield much authority over us choirboys; despite the fine education we received in the seminary, we had not quite shed the Viennese sense of mischief. He rehearsed the masses with us, very little of which we understood. In fact, Pius Richter and Rudolf Bibl, who at that time were the vice-directors of music to the Court, told us that their colleague Bruckner was a great man and that his masses were masterpieces – even better than those which they composed themselves! Yet with the disrespectful eyes of young boys we saw in Bruckner only the old, rather strange and above all extremely good-natured man, on whom we could carry out a whole string of pranks without fear of being punished.

The first thing which Bruckner used to do on arriving for a rehearsal was to look around, distressed, for a chair. 'Now lads, bring me a chair!' he would say, before sitting down slowly and awkwardly. Next he would put out his cigar. Thriftily, he stowed away the cheroot, which often was nothing more than a butt-end, in his jacket pocket. Then he would survey us, groaning in advance at the trouble we were about to cause him yet again. The lesson then began with the words, 'Now lads, let's get started!'

Once the rehearsal was over, the first thing he used to do was to search in his jacket for the remainder of his cigar. The search was almost always in vain, because one of our regular schoolboy pranks was to pinch the old man's beloved cigar from his jacket pocket. 'Oh Jesus,' he would say in despair, 'the carriage is down there waiting for me and I can't find my cigar!' In his wonderful innocence he would then ask us, 'Lads, help me find it!' This was all that we had been waiting for. We 'searched' for it, creating a tremendous din in the process, until, deeply touched, the old man would take the 'found' cigar from us, all the while thanking us repeatedly.

What entertained us most of all was the terrible nervousness which seemed to destroy Bruckner completely before the performance of one of his masses which he was to conduct. What did we know of his genius? We saw only a funny old man who, in his excitement, would hold the baton upside-down! In his other hand he would hold his large blue handkerchief, which he waved about like a flag in time to the music whilst he was conducting. Now and then he would beat time with his right hand whilst plunging his whole face into the handkerchief and blowing his nose laboriously. There were many things which amused us greatly.

Despite all this, I believe that we loved Anton Bruckner very much – and not simply for the three cakes he would treat us to after the performance of one of his masses. He went through thick and thin with his 'lads'; he was like a big child amongst us twelve- and thirteen-year-olds.

[Bruckner und die Sängerknaben, *Aus den Erinnerungen eines Wiener Philharmonikers*, reproduced in Grassberger and Partsch, *Bruckner – skizziert*, 137–9]

Holy Writ

Bruckner's studies with Simon Sechter left an imprint that lasted the rest of his life. He adhered to Sechter's principles as though they were articles of faith, in later years applying them obsessively to his own compositions – see, for instance, Max von Oberleithner on the revision of the First Symphony (p. 103). References to Sechter, in particular his harmonic theory, turn up frequently in the next set of reminiscences. In essence, Sechter's harmonic theory was based on Rameau's notion of a 'fundamental bass', a bass-line derived from the roots of the harmonies, moving in fourths or fifths; it need not be sounded, but it governs all harmonic progressions.

Bruckner's feeling that he was Sechter's inheritor can only have been strengthened when he succeeded him as Professor of Harmony and Counterpoint at the Vienna Conservatory in 1868. In 1875 he also took a lectureship at the Vienna University (despite determined opposition from the critic Eduard Hanslick), and there he continued to base his teaching solely on Sechter, as he did later in his private lessons – though, as we shall see, the style of his teaching could vary considerably. Some of Bruckner's pupils express surprise, even irritation, at this apparent narrowness; but scattered amongst their accounts – especially those of his private students – are valuable insights into Bruckner's compositional thinking.

ERNST DECSEY

The writer and critic Ernst Decsey (1870–1941) was born in Hamburg but spent most of his adult life in Vienna. Bruckner was to be one of his specialities, the subject of numerous articles and books, and of a play, *Der Musikant Gottes* ('God's Musician'), which he wrote with Victor Léon in 1924. Decsey entered the Vienna Conservatory in 1889, where he was one of

Bruckner's last theory pupils. This is his account of his first lesson. It shows how important Sechter's ideas still were to Bruckner (this was twenty-two years after Sechter's death), and how volatile the composer's temper could be.

Bruckner's classes began at one o'clock in the afternoon, exactly at the time of the *plenus venter*,* and continued until three o'clock. I stood, half-hidden behind the other pupils – those who had already been inducted – my heart beating loudly. Then, a few minutes after one, the door was flung open and on its threshold stood the Master before his pupils: he was dressed all in black – which gave him the appearance of a large, dark block – and was humbly swinging his wide floppy hat: 'Good morning, gentlemen!' Friendliness radiated from his broad, manly face; goodwill shone in his eyes – he climbed up to the lectern, his eyes scanned the young men, then he stopped suddenly. The radiance vanished from his face, it froze, then turned wild. He looked like a farmer who has just spotted a strange bull in his herd. And with a raucous, primitive voice, he let fly: 'Yes, you there, what do you want?' Silence filled the classroom, the students were rigid. With a shy, oboe-like voice, I began: 'I would like . . .' Whereupon Bruckner bellowed like a trombone: 'Yes, I would like what?' – I continued: ' . . . to join your class, Professor . . . I have already sat the entrance exam!' At this Bruckner became really wild: 'Entrance exam! With whom? It's got absolutely nothing to do with me! What they' – he pointed his thumb in the direction of the principals' office – 'have tested you on, those men from the *Conservatoire*' – he pronounced the word in a mock French accent – 'has got nothing to do with me!' And *in tempo più mosso*: 'Get out, get out, I don't need you here!'

At this point, the conversation temporarily ended. His strength boosted by rage, he took out his hat from behind his back and hit my face with the brim. My eye streamed, even today I can still feel the terrible pain.

But I stood my ground. At the age of twenty, one can be bold,

*Literally, 'full stomach', i.e. after lunch.

even with those whom one admires! 'Please, I have taken the entrance exam!' I said, ignoring the internal politics of the department.

At this point it seemed as if something had softened inside him. Perhaps in hitting me he also hurt himself, as do all good people who suffer from the pain they inflict on others. In short, the explosion was followed by a gesture which, despite still displaying signs of irritation, appeared yielding. His anger faded into mildness: 'You've got to be examined by me, do you understand? By me!' He looked at me commandingly, like Goliath: 'Go up there to the board! Now we'll see!'

He remained below and, pointing his index finger as if he were testing the faith of a heretic, stressing each syllable whilst winking slyly at the class, said: 'So – tell – me – this' – a pause – 'When – can – you – use – hid-den – fifths – cor-rect-ly?' He turned his back on me and winked at the class with the look of a good-natured mime artist: 'This'll catch him out.' Laughingly he muttered to himself: 'He'll soon be out of here, he can't know that!' I rejoiced inside. Yet I still showed nothing. Rapidly I scribbled the results of my coffee-house learning on the board: the hidden fifths, the intervals E–C, G–D; I explained, elucidated, explicated . . . one voice ascends by step, the other jumps to the dominant . . . the rules of harmony . . . Simon Sechter . . . I dropped the chalk and stood there, relaxed. The triumph of David!

A long silence. The class looked round the table. Bruckner remained silent, his jaw hanging open. He removed his hat. He rushed up to the board, wrapped his arms around me and rejoiced: 'You're the pearl of the century!' There was still a note of irony in his voice, but also delight over the miracle he had witnessed, satisfaction at my knowledge of Sechter, the Saint-Simon of theory – enough, he took me by the arm, led me down the steps and invited me to sit at the long table. I was admitted, accepted into the holy order, and told that I could, no, must in future sit at the right hand of the Master. Yes, Saint-Simon!* Bruckner's kind heart did not suspect the great fraud that was taking place. He nodded to the

*Decsey puns on Sechter's first name and that of the French philosopher Claude-Henri Saint-Simon (1760–1825).

others: 'The pearl of the century!' And that is how I was examined by Bruckner.

[Decsey, *Wie Anton Bruckner einem Schüller auf den Zahn fühlte*, as reproduced in *Bruckner – skizziert*, 105–6]

ALMA MAHLER

Once again, Alma Mahler's source for the following story appears to have been her husband, Gustav Mahler. Her opening disclaimer is endorsed by Mahler himself (below, p. 96) and by several of his friends and colleagues, but apparently Mahler did attend some of Bruckner's lectures while he was studying at Vienna University, where he may have experienced the following 'graphic' form of illustration for himself.

Strictly speaking, Bruckner was never Mahler's teacher, but he had respect for the young composer and encouraged him. There were some very strange stories about his teaching methods. These methods were highly naïve, but graphic. He would ask his pupils, 'Do you know what a suspension is? Well, look at this!' He took an enormous dirty handkerchief out of his trouser pocket. 'That's disgusting, eh? That's a dirty chord – a discord.' Then he pulled out a cleaner one. 'There, that's better – it's been resolved.' And finally, out came a snow-white handkerchief. 'Right, and now we're in the tonic.'

[Alma Mahler, 133–4]

FRIEDRICH KLOSE

Friedrich Klose's account of how he introduced himself to Bruckner has already been quoted ('Wide Trousers and Kid Gloves'). Klose now describes his audition – if that is quite the word – with Bruckner, and the style and content of his private lessons with Bruckner.

Like any young musician in my position, I believed that my compositions would be my most effective form of introduction. But what

Bruckner wanted above all was to look at my student exercises. He leafed through them, here and there lingering for some time, while I tried in vain to guess what he was thinking from the expression on his face. That made it all much clearer, he said at last, and now he would like to set me a little test; perhaps I would care to resolve the following harmonies – he wrote them down on a torn-off sheet of music paper – according to the strict rules. These were chords of the seventh in various inversions and positions. I didn't manage to resolve them all, the reason being Bruckner's remark that my student work had 'made it all much clearer'; for I was now terrified of creating consecutive fifths by suspension, or doubling the third in the root position, and I roundly declared such progressions to be unworkable. At any rate Bruckner must have been able to see from my exercises and from my explanations of the faulty resolutions that I was not musically illiterate, as he remarked that it was possible to build on what I had already learned. But if I would take his advice, I would start again at the beginning.

All of this fell like a cold shower on a 'symphonist' – one whose major works had already been performed – and I could not suppress a sense of wounded pride when Bruckner flatly refused even to glance at the score of my *Loreley*. However, I had come to Vienna with the intention of making a clean break with Genevan dilettantism and applying myself to sound learning, and so I fought back my displeasure and declared that I was prepared to begin again with the musical ABC. Bruckner, who had noted my momentary disappointment, felt that he should comfort me; he praised my resolution and assured me that I would not regret it, pointing out that he himself had carried on with his studies under Sechter's rigorous tuition until he was forty.

I now expected that an aural examination would follow, the kind of test my teacher Lachner* deemed indispensable in assessing a student's musical gifts: identification of keys and chords played at the piano. But nothing of the kind occurred. The examination was finished, and it only remained for me to ask about the terms

*Vinzenz Lachner (1811–1893), brother of the composer Franz Lachner (1803–1890).

of my private lessons. 'Yes,' said Bruckner gravely, a frown creasing his forehead, 'my lessons are very expensive.' I nerved myself for a prohibitive sum. 'Until recently,' he continued, 'I have asked three guilders per hour, but now' – he seemed almost embarrassed – 'I've had to raise it to five guilders.' Five guilders! That an artist of Bruckner's stature, in the cosmopolitan city of Vienna, should hesitate to ask for this, while out in the provinces insignificant piano teachers had the audacity to charge at least ten franks for their pedagogical key-bashing! It would have been laughable if it had not been so outrageous . . .

I had my first lesson with Bruckner on 5 February 1886. I still find it surprising that there was no aural test, and that he should have been content merely to set me a few harmonies to resolve – the kind of thing one can simply work out on paper without having to imagine every sound. My astonishment increased as I realized in the course of my studies that Bruckner attached little importance to external aural skills and none at all to perfect pitch. The explanation might be that he himself was able to picture sounds only by playing them, and for that reason composed at the piano, as I soon noticed. This gave me food for thought, for in Bruckner I now had an example of a composer who could create sublime works of art without perfect pitch, while Lachner, despite his infallible ear, could manage only dry, dead things . . .

The appointed times for my lessons were Wednesday evening at seven o'clock and Friday afternoon at one o'clock; they were never altered once in my three-and-a-half-year course, and they always began and ended exactly on the minute, even when that meant breaking off in the middle of a bar. Lateness brought a reprimand, and one might even find Bruckner waiting on the staircase, watch in hand, ready with this welcome: 'You're late, it's already five past one', or, 'Your watch must be slow'; these gently reproachful greetings were followed by apologies that the time lost could not be made up by prolonging the session. The lessons took place at the ink-blackened desk. Bruckner sat at the long side in a leather-upholstered armchair, his face turned towards the window; the pupil, to his right, at the end. First the relevant homework was examined thoroughly. If anything was wrong, Bruckner did not correct it himself; after making a few observations he handed it back for the student to labour over it. Meanwhile he might do some work of his own, perhaps amending a manuscript, or trying something out at the piano, without bothering about whether this distracted his companion. I cannot criticize Bruckner for treating the lessons so casually, for he was not the kind of composer who could produce his work, as it were, off the cuff; creation was hard for him, a fervent offering to his God brought forth at great cost, beside which teaching was a necessary but tiresome disturbance, the means by which he earned his daily bread. No one knows better than I do the spiritual exertion, the sheer expenditure of strength demanded by such creations, and how any distraction from 'high art' by trivialities – everyday matters that get in the way of the real issue – adds to the irritation of the nervous system.

After perusing the exercises, Bruckner would simply let the student work on for himself for the rest of the lesson, and it was only when he was specially requested, or when things went on too long, that he would take a look at one's work. The only time he himself wrote down a bar or two was when we came to a new stage in the course.

In Bruckner the teacher, Upper-Austrian coarseness was combined with Viennese warm-heartedness. His relationship with his pupils was that of the Master to his apprentices: Hans Sachs to David. Thus, even the best-motivated deviation from blind obedience was marked down as gross impertinence, which lead to many differences of opinion; nevertheless, these always ended in speedy reconciliation. Bruckner's gentle nature could not bear rancour for long.

One of the commonest expressions in the Master's vocabulary was '*Viechkerl*',* an exclamation which could admit at least as many nuances as might be possible on an organ with 120 stops. This word, when uttered with the chest-tone, *agitato*, conveyed annoyance; in the higher tenor register, *espressivo*, it expressed satisfaction at good results; in falsetto, with a pause on the '*ie*', *scherzando*, it had approximately the same meaning as 'clever beggar'. In between, as I have observed, were countless shades, reflecting the mood and circumstances.

* *Viech* ('animal', 'beast') plus *Kerl* ('chap', 'bloke').

Like any worthy musician of the old school, the Master always carried his snuff-box with him. At home it lay, ready for use, on the piano or on the desk. Bruckner did not indulge in snuff-taking with the same passion as Lachner, but an occasional pinch supplied his modest life-needs as did the occasional Upper-Austrian dish of smoked meat, and in the evenings a few Seidl beers from a plain, honest Bräuhaus.

It was a special honour, or at least a sign of approval, when Bruckner offered a pinch. To refuse would be to insult the venerable gentleman and would undoubtedly occasion a fall from grace. There was nothing for it but to put one's fingers in the box and convey the contents to the nose. At first, when Bruckner, acknowledging a good piece of work or wishing to stoke up my enthusiasm for a particularly challenging task, handed across the snuff-box with the words, 'Take a sniff first', I shrank from the pleasure. But one can get used to anything. In fact I soon came to see it as a set-back, not to say a privation, when the expected reward failed to materialize. Admittedly the quality of this brown stimulant was exceptionally fine. It comprised three different kinds of tobacco, which Frau Kathi knew how to blend in just the right proportions.

[Klose, 13–15, 27–8 and 94–6]

> Klose's initial reaction to Bruckner's 'Back to Basics' teaching-method was apparently not unique. But despite the warmth in his later description of the man, his verdict on Bruckner the teacher does not appear to have softened with time.

With Bruckner, it was neither incompetence, nor laziness, nor malice that made him hold fast to such a bloodless system, rather, as I have already said, simple respect for the theorist Sechter. But even if Bruckner had been free of this belief in authority, this dead weight imposed on progressive thinking, it would still have been hard to imagine him as one of the reformers, those whose goal it is to tear things down and build afresh. Such audacity was completely contrary to Bruckner's respectful nature . . .

It is certainly true to say that Bruckner's teaching method was focused too narrowly on theoretical considerations. I heard this view expressed by Franz Schalk who, as is well known, was also a Bruckner pupil. When I told him that I had now arrived at three-part counterpoint, he observed that the time had come to ask me whether I intended to devote myself to composition or to becoming a Kapellmeister; if the latter were the case, then he would advise me to give up theoretical studies in favour of a more practical training. I did not take his advice, but I will not speculate here as to whether this was a help or a hindrance to my future artistic development. For the benefit of teachers and students, I will merely offer the following maxim:

Salvation lies in practice,
Not in theory!

[Klose, 85–7]

FERDINAND LÖWE

Ferdinand Löwe (1865–1925) attended the Bruckner's classes at the Vienna Conservatory, and later got to know the composer more intimately as a member of his 'Gaudeamus' circle. As a conductor, he was an enthusiastic Bruckner champion. He also helped Franz Schalk prepare piano arrangements of several of the symphonies. Unfortunately, his enthusiasm did not prevent him from taking liberties with Bruckner's music: in his 'edition' of the Ninth Symphony (the first to appear in print, seven years after the composer's death), Bruckner's orchestration is Wagnerized and his daring harmonies bowdlerized. Nevertheless, Löwe's defence of Bruckner as teacher is loyal and impassioned.

There is a widely held opinion that Bruckner was, if not an extremely bad teacher, then certainly not a good one; if anything, this view is even more persistent today. Of course, those who were able to listen to his lectures – amongst them some important musicians of the recent past – knew differently. Admittedly, drumming into untalented students the most fundamental aspects of harmony and counterpoint as quickly as possible was not his forte. However, truly gifted pupils could hardly have wished for a more magnificent teacher. Simply the fact that the 'teacher' in him was constantly complemented by the 'artist' made his teaching unique. Bruckner was never satisfied with a piece of work which merely fulfilled all the rules of counterpoint. At best, his praise would be limited to 'Quite good, but the voice-leading could be a lot better.' If, on the other hand, a pupil let his imagination run a little too wildly, then, mixing praise with caution once again, he would say: 'Yes, that's good! I like that! We can do that later! But we're in school now; and here you've got to keep strictly to the rules!'

[Göllerich/Auer, 4/1, 67]

FRIEDRICH ECKSTEIN

A more even-handed, but still fundamentally positive view of Bruckner the teacher comes from Friedrich Eckstein, who studied with Bruckner both privately and in his classes at the University. Eckstein reacts strongly against what he calls 'unclear, one-sided or simply wrong' ideas about Bruckner the teacher. His account of the causes of Bruckner's theoretical dogmatism is sympathetic, and towards the end of this extract there is a delightful illustration of how, for Bruckner, strict schooling could even be an aid to artistic freedom.

Most assessments of Bruckner as teacher do not consider sufficiently how closely his teaching methods were bound up with his singular, curious life-story, or how the circumstances of his life explain not only the unique depth and logical consistency of those methods, but also their difficulty of access.

For Bruckner, recognition did not come until relatively late, and even then it was only after indescribable hardships and struggles, only after a whole lifetime of hard work and the most bitter privations.

He often told me about his young days as assistant to the village schoolmaster in the Upper Austrian village of Windhaag, when sheer poverty had frequently forced him to spend the whole night playing dance music for the farmers for just a silver twenty-shilling piece, and of the infinite effort that had been demanded of him until, by degrees, he had become organist at St Florian, then cathedral organist in Linz, and finally Hofkapelle organist and professor at the Conservatory in Vienna.

It was as a direct consequence of this hard schooling that Bruckner would tolerate no weakness either in himself or in anyone else, and just as he had formed his artistry thoroughly from the basic elements in constant, intense struggle with the most intractable forces, so he now demanded from his students a secure technique, firmly built on the unshakeable logic of the craft and on tried and tested foundations.

For Bruckner, whose whole musical output was sustained by the basic sentiment '*Non confundar in aeternam*',* music was the mysterious revelation of highest things; thus he saw his teaching as a sacred, priestly office, which he was resolved to perform in purity and with unrelenting rigour.

For this reason, he could be brusquely dismissive of any 'flights of genius' on the part of his pupils. It was the same with any others who brought him laughably bad or stale compositions; time and time again these unfortunate would-be composers ended up taking to their heels in fear or with their pride deeply wounded. In such cases Bruckner would always insist that no one should be allowed to bother him with such creations until they had mastered the rules; that way, he would be spared the trouble of having to criticize or repair defective compositions.

And just as Albrecht Dürer and other great Masters would first instruct their pupils solely in the art of preparing the colours, the mixing and the application of the ground before they were allowed to paint, so Bruckner's young hopefuls were expected to devote themselves for years to the fundamentals of harmony and strict classical style before earning the right to free composition. Bruckner's curriculum was based on a painstakingly contrived system, rooted in time-honoured, traditional practice, in which the basic harmonies and their constituent parts move and combine according to certain laws, to which the free fall of natural bodies provides a curious analogy. And from these basic principles one could system-

*'Let me never be confounded' – the final words of the *Te Deum*. Bruckner uses a setting of this phrase from his own *Te Deum* as the basis for the final climax of the Adagio of his Seventh Symphony.

atically derive the contrapuntal treatment of the part-writing, and so on, to ever freer and bolder formulations.

This explains why the Master would often get very angry when an impatient student pestered him with questions, far in advance of the stage he had reached. 'Follow me closely, with trust and patience, and you'll understand this all for yourself when the time is right; you'll learn a thousand times better that way than if I answer all these nervy questions' – this was something I often heard him say in cases like these.

And so it happened that the students who committed themselves to this strictly organized course of instruction gradually gained confidence and became initiated in the subtleties and profound 'mysteries' of classical composition, so little understood by many other musicians. Thus a Bruckner pupil could sometimes automatically produce chordal sequences which recalled the incomparable arpeggiated harmonies of J. S. Bach's *Chromatic Fantasy*.

Again and again, Bruckner insisted that strict composition was the foundation of all free style, and that anyone who failed to Master it would never be able to rise above mediocrity. Even in the boldest harmonic progressions of Richard Wagner, one could clearly discern the same unrelentingly strict classical logic.

Bruckner loved to illustrate his musical theories with graphic comparisons from everyday life, and I still remember clearly how he explained the relationship between strict and free composition with this choice analogy: 'Think of a genteel English lord, a man who moves quite freely in polite society and can take the odd liberty and get away with it because everyone's quite sure that he's still a man of exquisite breeding, while an uncultivated bumpkin has to keep watching himself all the time. In the same way, a musician who's thoroughly schooled in strict composition can allow himself all kinds of daring touches which the less-educated man would draw back from in terror.'

Anyone who would not or could not submit himself to Bruckner's rigorous system would simply not be taken on, and the Master was far from devastated when some conceited youth, loudly confident of his own talent, went elsewhere. This was not, as has sometimes been alleged, the expression of a schoolmasterly pedantry, rather a sign of the tremendous artistic strength of this great composer, who would make no concession to any misconceived '*galant*' style or shallow craving for novelty.

[Eckstein, 156–9]

MAX VON OBERLEITHNER

For Max von Oberleithner, there were other ways in which a pupil might learn from Bruckner: ways unconnected with his theoretical ideas or teaching methods.

The steady unfolding of Bruckner's teaching meant that there was never any danger that something too difficult would suddenly be demanded; on the contrary, progress was rather too slow: this was a good, thorough system, requiring several years. There were no references to the classical masterworks. I would often go to collect Bruckner from the University, and I remember him mentioning in one of his lessons that the harmonic fundamentals could also be identified throughout the works of Wagner, adding – to encourage me – that proving this might make an enticing project. But I resolved that Wagner's lucid, vivid creations would never be dissected by me!

This separation of theoretical study and artistic creation explains why Bruckner's students never went to him for guidance or advice concerning their own works. But this lack was more than made up for by the opportunities one had to observe Bruckner himself at composition. I myself was able to follow the revision of the First Symphony, the composition of *Psalm 150* for the Gesellschaft Concert and the choral work *Helgoland* for the Vienna Männergesangverein. What interested me most, however, was watching the sketching-out of the Ninth Symphony – Bruckner was only too happy to play from the work in progress, without anyone having to ask him. This was more a case of reading than of listening, as his fingers trembled and in his nervousness he usually played the important entries twice; but one could still make out the basic idea quite clearly.

On one occasion Bruckner played through the theme of the Adagio several times because he couldn't make it out properly (it was covered with corrections), so I wrote it out neatly and brought it to him at our next lesson. It was in B major, and at one point – in the seventh bar – there was a strong resemblance to the Grail motif from *Parsifal.* By then he had completely transformed it, making its shape more significant. All that survived was the rhythm of the first bar and the rising phrase that recalled the Grail motif. The melodic step D♯–G♯ in the upper voice at the first bar had become a great sigh, B–C (a ninth).

This enlarging of the melodic step was typical of Bruckner. In fact, he was the first symphonist to lay out his leading themes over several octaves, as for instance in the opening theme of the Seventh (E major) Symphony. One sees the same tendency in Richard Strauss, as a comparison of the main theme of *Heldenleben* with that of Beethoven's *Eroica* Symphony clearly shows.

Sechter's theory may be neccessary as a foundation, but I learned much more by watching the construction of Bruckner's Ninth Symphony, and especially from the copying out of the finale of the Eighth Symphony from the original manuscript, which the Master entrusted to me. I still remember those wonderful times when the different strands in the development of this colossal movement gradually became clear. As great mountains emerge in full splendour when the sun banishes the mist, so the score itself blossomed ever more richly, and all so-called formal logic vanished like mist before the light of love for these revelations of the innermost heart. The experience of getting to know this score, without ever hearing it at the piano, transformed my admiration for Bruckner into rapturous devotion.

One can imagine how much there was to learn from this score. It should be stressed that all his students, including those at the Conservatory, had the opportunity to further their education, perhaps not during their schooldays, but certainly later – provided their talent and admiration for Bruckner were genuine. By studying the then unpublished scores of the symphonies and masses, they grew to maturity; sometimes they were even able to give the Master advice. I am thinking particularly of Josef and Franz Schalk and Ferdinand Löwe, and earlier on Gustav Mahler, who made the four-hand piano arrangement of the Third Symphony with Krzyzanowski. This relationship between Master and pupil was also valuable for Bruckner, because his students were his first audience, and those whose talents ripened as they worked with his scores were to become his finest interpreters in the concert hall.

[Oberleithner, 27–30]

> For those who know what Löwe and Franz Schalk were to do in their notorious 'editions' of Bruckner's works, the remarks in Oberleithner's final paragraph may have an ominous ring – what kind of 'advice' is he talking about? The section on the Bruckner circle, 'Gaudeamus', contains some answers, though it also raises difficult questions. Another name mentioned by Oberleithner is Gustav Mahler (1860–1911), who as a Bruckner champion has had a rather better press, though his attitude to Bruckner's music was not uncritical, and with regard to texts he was certainly no purist.

GUSTAV MAHLER

I was never one of Bruckner's pupils. People must say that I was because I could often be seen with him and, in any case, I was one of his particular admirers and supporters. I even believe that at that time I was, together with my friend Krzyzanowski (who is now working in Vienna), the only one. I think this was during the years 1875 to 1881. His letters to me were written in various years and say really very little. I do not think you would do such a man a service by publishing these documents. Anyway, whoever has ears and eyes can also hear and see. My contact with him lasted until the completion of his Seventh Symphony. I can still remember with pleasure how one morning, during a lecture at the university, he called me out of the lecture theatre (to the astonishment of my colleagues) and played the wonderful theme of the Adagio to me on a very dusty piano – you know yourself what Bruckner was like. He had an untainted happiness, which at that time was youthful, almost childlike, as well as an inherently trusting nature. Thus, despite the large gap between us, we had a friendly relationship. It was therefore natural that I should develop both a knowledge and a recognition of his life and goals, which in turn did not remain without influence on my educational development as both an artist and an individual. And so I may, with more right than most, call myself his 'pupil', and I will always do this in grateful admiration.

[Göllerich/Auer, 4/1, 448–9 *fn*]

FELIX VON KRAUS

Felix von Kraus was another of Bruckner's university students. Where Max von Oberleithner played down the significance of Bruckner's theoretical teaching, Kraus virtually dismisses it, describing the composer's lectures as 'an artistic delicacy of the very highest quality, which completely overshadowed their educational content'. The remark attributed to Bruckner about the importance of 'sounds' is striking, given Friedrich Klose's assertion that Bruckner 'attached little importance to external aural skills' (p. 38): but then, after Klose, Kraus's version of Bruckner the teacher is almost unrecognizable. Felix von Kraus's memories of Bruckner's lectures are summarized by his daughter, Felicitas von Kraus.

Bruckner would address a few enlightening thoughts to his 'dear students', and then write the relevant music example on the blackboard, adding, 'My dear students, always remember that with music the important thing is that you hear the *sounds*, and don't just read the notes, and I don't know yet whether that's the case with all of you when you read off the blackboard. So perhaps it's better if I play it for you!' That said, he would sit at the piano and then no more reading would be done that day, because the sound would immediately distract him from the subject they were supposed to be studying and, having finished one example, he would move straight on to another one. Sometimes, oblivious of time and place, he would abandon himself completely to the spell of his genius, with the words 'Now, my dear students, I must just play you what I've written in the last few days!' The notes would then rain down in floods over the captivated listeners, the performance often punctuated by divinely naïve observations on the link between the creative act and his physical condition – until the two allotted hours were over and the bell rang, calling him and his audience back from another world; whereupon he would apologize briefly for his forgetfulness, leaving the listeners with the feeling that they had been torn away from a magical dream.

[Kraus, 17–18]

GUIDO ADLER

Guido Adler (1855–1941) has been described as 'the father of modern musicology', and with some justice. In such pioneering essays as *Umfang, Methode und Ziel der Musikwissenschaft* ('The Range, Method and Goal of Musicology', 1885), he effectively defined the principles of musicology as we know it today. Adler studied theory with Bruckner at the Vienna Conservatory (1868–74), then read law at the University before eventually deciding to commit himself to music. In 1896 he succeeded Hanslick at the Vienna University, where his pupils included the composers Anton [von] Webern and Egon Wellesz and the Bruckner scholars Alfred Orel and Robert Haas. Alder wrote influential studies of many of the important figures in Viennese music, from Haydn to his friend Mahler. The essay *Anton Bruckners Stellung in der Musikgeschichte* ('Anton Bruckner's position in the History of Music') is largely an objective appraisal of the composer, but Alder does allow a little space for personal recollection.

Bruckner was either unable or unwilling to relate theory to practice; all he could do was hold fast to the basic principles. When, in the course of one of his lectures, he explained one of these rules to us, he would often leave the lectern and walk over to the blackboard, smile quietly and whisper to himself, as though in secret, 'When I'm not here I do things differently.' He lacked the theoretical means to bring practice into his teaching. Or was it that his respect for the laws of musical theory was as deep as his veneration for the teachings of the Church? In the schoolroom things progressed automatically; in his artistic creations he was a true embodiment of the Naïve in the Schillerian sense.* He looked out on the world like an innocent child, with clear, bright eyes; and if, in his down-to-earth country (or, to be frank, peasant-like) way he suspected that some mischief was being perpetrated, he would screw up his eyes as though to say, 'Look, you can't fool me, and I can just as easily turn the tables on you.'

[Kobald, 10–11]

How could the style of Bruckner's teaching have varied so radically? Max von Oberleithner, who studied with the composer both privately and at the University, offers a partial answer in the next extract. There remains the question of how to reconcile descriptions of Bruckner the pedagogue and Bruckner the improviser, the creator of inspired 'fantasies'. Friedrich Eckstein has already given us the composer's own, highly entertaining explanation of how respect for the rules may still allow 'daring touches'; Oberleithner concludes with a still more striking image.

MAX VON OBERLEITHNER

It is quite true that Bruckner's manner of teaching differed according to whether he was at the Conservatory or the University; but I did not study with him at the Conservatory, and I restrict myself to personal experience.

As our work at the University was not inspected, Bruckner could limit himself to stimulating our appetites. He used stories to spice up his lectures. Amongst other things, he offered an observation on the different characters of the triads.

The chord on the first degree in C major, said Bruckner, expressed joy; that of the second, sorrow. The chord on the third degree was the lyricist. E minor was 'for the ladies' to compose in. With the

*In his essay *Über naïve und sentimentalische Dichtung* ('On naïve and sentimental poetry'), the German poet, playwright, historian and critic Friedrich Schiller (1759–1805) contrasts the 'naïve' poet, who is at one with Nature, with the 'sentimental' modern poet, who is separated from Nature and yearns to be reunited with it. These two concepts and their antitheses were influential in many different strands of nineteenth-century German thought.

fourth degree, we were again on a major chord, though not like the Generalissimus on the first degree, which Bruckner also compared with the Trinity. For Bruckner, F sharp minor was full of longing, F minor melancholic, while A minor he described as gentle. D minor, his favourite key, was solemn, mysterious.* On this occasion he remarked, 'I'll write my last symphony in D minor, just like Beethoven's Ninth. Beethoven won't object.'

In his private lessons one worked seriously and conscientiously. Bruckner demanded the same diligence and patience from his students that he had always maintained himself, and his eagerness to learn was extraordinary. Sechter's theory, the sole content of the lessons, was an almost religious doctrine to him, not to be questioned. Of course, this was only the foundation, not for the art of composition itself, which took the rules for granted but was ruled only by imagination: he once told me, 'You can compose as you like!' He held to this in his works; however, in his sketches he would often indicate the so-called fundamentals of the harmonies in tiny letters, as though this imparted a theoretical rectitude to the more complicated passages. In this he was like a bold interpreter of the Holy Scriptures who never completely disregards the basic idea.

[Oberleithner, 24–5]

*'solemn, mysterious': *feierlich, mysteriös* – the marking for the first movement of the Ninth Symphony is *Feierlich, Misterioso* . . .

A Great and Painstaking Pleasure

'He was like a bold interpreter of the Holy Scriptures who never completely disregards the basic idea.' The more one knows about how Bruckner composed, the more appropriate Max von Oberleithner's closing image seems. The struggle between a powerful imagination and an equally powerful compulsion to prove 'theoretical rectitude' – between the spirit and the letter of the law – is evident on page after page of Bruckner's manuscripts. As August Stradal says, Bruckner may have improvised 'purely to give pleasure', but it is doubtful whether he ever achieved the same ease and spontaneity in written composition. And yet that very tension could be a vital creative force. Oberleithner noted that Bruckner marked harmonic fundamentals in his sketches; Friedrich Eckstein confirms this, and adds more detail. Although the process appears laborious, it obviously did not rule out poetic inspiration.

FRIEDRICH ECKSTEIN

Almost every time I visited Bruckner at his apartment in the Hessgasse, I found him sitting at his old-fashioned, bulky Bösendorfer grand piano, deep in the sketch of one of his symphonies, laboriously, with shaking hands, coaxing out the harmonies. These musical outlines were in themselves quite remarkable. As a rule, only the violin or the top woodwind line was filled in, and at the bottom, the bass; in between was a yawning gap, and it wasn't until much later that the remaining orchestral voices were added. The harmonic dimension and the arrangement of the orchestral voices were already clearly established in the Master's inner ear, and here and there, underneath the bass-line, would stand a note, usually in the form of a capital letter, to indicate the harmonic 'fundamental tone' of the passage in question.

But what a wealth of unimagined beauty was revealed when I saw the very first bars of one newly begun work, the wonderful

Seventh Symphony: where the string tremolos launch a deeply moving harmonic sequence that arches through a splendid chain of suspensions, bathing the main theme, on horn and cellos, in shafts of radiant sunlight!

Bruckner enjoyed playing what he had just composed, especially when he was at home – sometimes to his complete circle of friends, and often to me alone. This was particularly the case with the Seventh Symphony, which at that time was still incomplete.

Over the years, I had the special good fortune to hear Bruckner play through almost the whole of the Seventh Symphony and later the Eighth, and to hear his comments on them. It was the same with the *Te Deum* and several other of his works. Beside the regular tuition in harmonic and contrapuntal theory, I was therefore allowed to experience the conception and gradual construction of these works. If the reader considers how Bruckner's comments on this or that passage, his occasional remarks on the characteristics and purpose of the harmonies, the themes and the orchestration of his compositions, enabled me to probe them so deeply, he will surely imagine the states of rapture and blissful devotion attained by Bruckner's young pupil.

[Eckstein, 149–50]

There may have been moments when the demands of the imagination got the better of Bruckner's sense of propriety – see, for instance, Eckstein on the composition of the Adagio of the Eighth Symphony (pp. 104–6): but there were undoubtedly times when anxiety about theoretical correctness dominated, as the next reminiscence confirms. Bruckner had in fact begun the Ninth Symphony in 1887, but work was seriously held up by full-scale revisions of the Third, Eighth and First Symphonies. The revised scores of No. 3, and particularly No. 8, are still the objects of impassioned controversy, but nowadays most Bruckner commentators regard the reworking of Symphony No. 1 as a deplorable waste of time – it certainly softens some of the 'boldness' of the original conception.

MAX VON OBERLEITHNER

Bruckner had good cause to be disgruntled that winter, as none of his works was performed either in Vienna or in Germany, even though he had reached his sixty-fifth year and finished his Eighth Symphony. At the time he was working on a revision of the First Symphony. Ferdinand Löwe had played the symphony to the Court Kapellmeister Hans Richter, who promptly took the score away with him with the intention of performing it as soon as possible. But Bruckner insisted on looking through the score once more before it was heard in public. The result of this decision was another year's work. He was delighted with the boldness of the symphony's conception, comparing it to a sharp-tongued old hag and giving it the name 'Das Beserl'.* But he also noted that many parts of it might prove difficult, and he felt he had to study them closely; and thus began his mania for searching out so-called consecutive fifths and octaves. The work added to his nervous irritation, as it later did when he was writing the Ninth Symphony.

[Oberleithner, 32]

CARL ALMEROTH

Carl Almeroth now reveals that, for Bruckner, the need to reconcile imagination and the rules was not the only source of tension in written composition.

When Bruckner was orchestrating one of his symphonies, a powerful struggle began to take place in the Master's soul. He would strike some chords ten to twenty times over, whilst at the same time going over in his mind the range of different instruments to which he could allocate particular notes. Striking the same note, the same harmony, over and over again seemed monotonous to us, but it enabled Bruckner to make difficult decisions about the effect of the tone-colour. Working with meticulous accuracy, giving each

*From the German *Besen*, a 'broom'. A possible English equivalent would be the virtually obsolete 'besom', meaning either a stiff broom or, in Oberleithner's words, 'a sharp-tongued old hag' – a battleaxe.

note the correct sound – for Bruckner, this was a great and 'painstaking' pleasure. For this reason, his scores will always remain exemplary models for coming musical generations.

When Bruckner was composing or sketching one of his works, things moved a lot more quickly, but also more quietly. Indeed, his musical fantasy was so magnificent that even his opponents maintained for some while that he was truly a fountain of ideas, and that another composer could have made six symphonies from one of Bruckner's.

Göllerich/Auer, 2/1, 303–4]

FRIEDRICH ECKSTEIN

Friedrich Eckstein briefly described the experience of looking over Bruckner's shoulder while he was writing the Seventh Symphony. He continues with a more detailed account of the composition of the Eighth. Amongst other valuable insights, Eckstein's account shows that there were times when Bruckner was prepared – after some deliberation – to yield to imaginative pressure and break his own rules.

At that time Bruckner spent many hours each day composing his Eighth Symphony. The working out of the first movements took the whole of that winter, and it wasn't until the spring of 1885 that the Adagio was finished.

What an overwhelming experience it was, the first time Bruckner took up the sketch and played me the main theme of the first movement: the incomparable harmonic and rhythmic boldness of the bass-figure repeatedly broken by breathtaking pauses, moving outwards beneath the mysteriously shimmering pianissimo-tremolo of the strings! And then the development of that tremendous movement! One evening, the Master showed me the freshly written conclusion, in which that great theme dies away; and as he played me this passage, in which pulse and breath seem to grow ever weaker, I observed that Bruckner's expression was changing, that the corners of his mouth were sinking and his body had begun to shudder. As he played, he bent towards me and said, almost inaudibly: 'This is Death's clock, that ticks for everyone, and never stops ticking till all is past!'*

Bruckner worked long and hard on the wonderful Adagio in D flat major, and whenever I came to him during that period he played me whatever he had just written. One such occasion deserves special mention. All the time that I had known him, in our evening conversations amongst his friends or during my own lessons, I had heard him declare repeatedly that there was no place for the harp in a true symphony. Liszt of course had used the instrument very effectively, but his creations were tone-paintings, programme music, symphonic poems, not genuine symphonies in the strictest sense. For this reason Bruckner had absolutely renounced the sound of the harp in his own symphonies.

Before long, though, I got the impression that at some point in the Adagio he had reached an impasse, as it was several weeks since he had last spoken of his work or played me anything from it. Then one day I arrived for my lesson to find the Master in unusually high spirits. I was scarcely in the hallway when he cried: 'Samiel, I've put harps in the Adagio! I just had to, there was no other way!'

After a few words 'justifying' himself, he sat at the piano and played to me the newly reworked Adagio right from the beginning. I listened, deeply moved, to the solemn entry of the three harps, and as they spread their magical sounds over the stately chorus of string voices, they seemed to lift the movement above all earthly things.

When Bruckner got up from the piano we both sank into a long,

*Eckstein's chronology presents a problem: the date in the first paragraph and the account of the inclusion of the harps in the Adagio make it clear that, in general, Eckstein is talking about the first version of the Eighth Symphony (1884–7); however, in that original version the first movement does not end with the quiet, 'Death's clock' passage, but continues for another twenty-nine bars, *fff*, reaching a resounding conclusion in C major. It is in the revised score (1887–90) that the movement ends as Eckstein describes. Did his memory confuse the order of events? Whatever the case, the 'Death's clock' image is confirmed by Johann Kerschagl, who recollects that Bruckner referred to the first movement's final climax (letter V–W) as 'The Annunciation of Death' (*Todverkündung*), and to the following coda as 'Death's clock' (*Totenuhr*): 'This is like when someone is lying on his deathbed, and opposite him hangs the clock, and while his life comes to its end it goes on beating steadily; tick, tock, tick, tock . . .' [Göllerich/Auer, 4/3, 15] silent reverie. Finally, without saying a word, I folded my hands in a gesture of entreaty. Bruckner understood, sat down again at the instrument, and played the whole Adagio through once more.

So, apart from the Master himself, I must surely be the first mortal to have heard these incomparably sublime, psalm-like sounds!

The composition of a new work demanded all Bruckner's reserves of strength, and he suffered more than ever from the burden of his official duties, which robbed him of far too much time and energy. So his whole nervous system grew increasingly irritated, and this sometimes expressed itself in strange forms.

I still remember him working on the Scherzo of the symphony during that terribly hot summer, and how almost every time I visited him he played something for me and was delighted by my enthusiasm. And just as all his friends had received special nicknames, so he gave pet names to his themes; for him, they were living beings with their own particular destinies.

One of his favourite themes he called 'Zizipeh', because it reminded him of a titmouse's call; I have already mentioned the 'Death's Clock'; another was the 'Beserl', and the stubbornly recurring theme of the Scherzo of the Eighth Symphony he named 'Deutscher Michel', or, more affectionately, his 'Michi'.*

[Eckstein, 144–6]

JULIUS BAYER

Dr Julius Bayer, organist and choirmaster in Steyr, was the son of Julia and Franz Xaver Bayer, with whom the older Bruckner regularly spent part of his annual summer holiday. Bayer recorded this recollection for a

*For *Beserl*, see p. 103. For the origin of Eckstein's Brucknerian nickname 'Samiel', see p. 117. *Deutscher Michel* is defined by *The Oxford Companion to German Literature* as a 'proverbial figure of easy-going good nature and simple-mindedness'. His first recorded appearance is in a collection of proverbs, *Die deutschen Sprichwörter* by Sebastian Franck (1499–1542). By the nineteenth century, *Deutscher Michel* had become a popular figure with cartoonists and satirists. Could Bruckner's invocation of *Deutscher Michel* indicate a degree of ironic self-awareness? The identification of the Scherzo theme with *Deutscher Michel* is again confirmed by Kerschagl.

BBC2 *Workshop* documentary, *OAMDG* in 1968, not long before his death. Bruckner was on such close terms with Julius Bayer's mother that a rumour grew, one which Bayer himself did not seem too anxious to quash: he told the programme's director, Barrie Gavin, 'Anton Bruckner was a close friend of my father; some say he was an even closer friend of my mother.' But Bayer's anecdote avoids this delicate issue.

I was lucky enough to know the great composer when I was a small boy, and I can just remember sitting on his knee when he visited my family. Bruckner used to come and stay with my father and mother between 1888 and 1893, and it was here, in Steyr, that he wrote a good deal of the Eighth Symphony.* He had the reputation of being a rather simple man. I remember my father telling me how he went to see the composer one day when he was working on the symphony in our house. He could hear Bruckner trying out a theme on the piano, and so he didn't disturb him. Instead, my father noted down the theme and went to try it out on the church organ. After a while Bruckner came into the church and heard what was being played. Of course he got into a terrible state. 'Where did you hear that?' he said. My father wanted to tease him, and replied, 'Oh, somewhere in Vienna; I don't know – perhaps a band played it in the park.' Bruckner then fell on his knees before the altar, crying out: 'God forgive me! I have stolen another man's music without knowing it!'

Then naturally my father had to put him out of his misery and told him the truth. 'You scoundrel!' shouted the composer in his broad Upper-Austrian dialect. 'But never mind. Let's go and have a glass of Pilsner together. I forgive you.'

[*Workshop*: *Anton Bruckner – OAMDG*, BBC2 1968]

*The original score of the Eighth Symphony was completed in 1887; at the time Bayer mentions, Bruckner would have been working on the revised version (1887–90).

ALEXANDER FRÄNKEL

Bruckner may have been horrified at the thought of unconsciously stealing someone else's tune, but he was quite capable of turning to others for advice or ideas when composing, as the next two reminiscences confirm (see also the section on the Bruckner circle, 'Gaudemus'). Fränkel's remark about Bruckner's 'deliberate analogy' to Beethoven confirms Max von Oberleithner's report (p. 100); his final sentence is especially thought-provoking.

Now and then Bruckner also honoured me with an insight into his musical plans. I had no cause to feel proud of this, as he often told me how he repeatedly called on the artistic judgement of his renowned housekeeper Kathi, offering up musical ideas for her expert assessment. She seems, incidentally, to have been in agreement with everything. I can also testify that he wrote nine symphonies as a deliberate analogy to Beethoven – he told me expressly that he wanted to emulate Beethoven in this respect. The composition of an opera was certainly not beyond the realms of his future intentions; it was merely a question of finding the right story – his preference was for a text with a 'mystical hero like Lohengrin'.

[Göllerich/Auer, 4/2, 29–30]

KARL WALDECK

Bruckner's organist friend Karl Waldeck from Linz remembers an occasion when his criticism of a work in progress was taken very seriously by the composer.

Even while I was still a trainee teacher I realized that Bruckner had a great talent for the organ. I went to him for lessons for which, as the son of a penniless country schoolmaster, I paid fifty crowns an hour; I also stood in for him at Benediction in both churches (the Old Cathedral and the Parish Church). Once I forgot to turn up for Benediction, which angered Bruckner so much that he refused to go on teaching me. My great interest in his playing, plus the fact that I used my position to recommend him as a piano teacher, restored me to his favour. I went to all the services to hear him play, and I made it a habit to collect him from Vespers and go for a walk with him. If the weather was bad we would go to his home and he would play me sketches from his compositions, most of which gave no more than the upper and lower voices in outline. One day Bruckner played me the sketch of the Credo from the F minor Mass, after which he asked me for my opinion. I said that I did not think the Et incarnatus was on the same level as the rest of the Credo. After thinking for a moment, Bruckner said, 'What about this then?' and he improvised the tenor solo at a higher pitch with an accompaniment in quavers, which we both found much more satisfactory, and he immediately wrote it down and kept it.

[Gräflinger, 114]

But not all those from whom Bruckner sought advice were as sympathetic, or as apparently helpful as Karl Waldeck.

HEINRICH SCHENKER

The writings of the Austrian theorist Heinrich Schenker (1868–1935) have exerted a powerful influence on musical analysis in the twentieth century. According to Schenker, the great tonal works reveal structural layers: foreground, middle ground and background – the latter expressed in terms resembling a conventional I–V–I tonal cadence, with the top line falling by step to the tonic.* Schenker studied harmony and counterpoint with Bruckner at the Vienna Conservatory in the years 1887–9. Although he expressed admiration for Bruckner as a teacher, Schenker's feelings about Bruckner the composer were more complicated. For Schenker, Bruckner was 'too much a foreground composer', a cultivator of great moments rather than a

*Or as an exasperated student friend of this writer put it, 'If you believe Schenker, all the classics are basically "Three Blind Mice".'

creator of sustained symphonic arguments; though it is also evident that Schenker was impressed by some of those 'moments'. The following brief reminiscence is taken from a letter to the Bruckner-apologist August Halm.

Once – in class – Bruckner called me over to the piano. 'Listen to this, Herr Schenker,' he said, and played me part of something, obviously a climactic passage. 'Do you think that's enough, or should I take it further?' As to what might have gone before or after, of that I heard nothing. Later, I discovered that it was part of the Seventh Symphony, which Bruckner was working on at the time. But how could he ask a question like that? How could anyone judge rightly from what he played – and what does his question tell us about his own judgement?

[Letter to August Halm, 3 April 1924 – reproduced in *Heinrich Schenkers Bruckner-Verstandnis*, by Helmut Federhofer – Archiv für Musikwissenschaft XXXIX Jahrgang, Heft 3, 1982, 3. Quartal, 210]

Gaudeamus

Few composers have been as susceptible to the influence of friends and colleagues as Bruckner. It is one of the factors that makes editing his manuscripts such a nightmarish task. Commentators sometimes express a pious hope that Bruckner's scores might one day be purged of the influence of 'well-meaning but uncomprehending friends' (as more than one writer has put it). But as several reminiscences have already shown. Bruckner made a point of playing his works to friends as he wrote them, soliciting their advice, and sometimes making significant changes to the music in response. Some of this advice is recorded (for instance, by Karl Waldeck), but one may safely presume that a great deal more of it is not. Purging 'original' Bruckner completely of external influences would probably require supernatural insight.

But are those influences only to be deplored? Who is to say that Karl Waldeck's criticism of the Et incarnatus from the F minor Mass was unjustified? As we shall see, one or two of the suggestions apparently made by members of Bruckner's intimate circle of friends resulted in changes that critics and performers have largely approved. Moreover, given the neglect and devastating criticism to which Bruckner was subjected during his Vienna period, it is doubtful whether his will to compose would have survived as it did without the help and encouragement of at least some of those friends.

Bruckner's nickname for his intimate circle was 'Gaudeamus', a reference to the old student song, 'Gaudeamus igitur' ('Let us therefore rejoice'), probably best known today as the tune that concludes the *Academic Festival Overture*, Op. 80, by Bruckner's arch-rival Brahms. As many of the regular members of 'Gaudeamus' were originally his students, the nickname is particularly appropriate. Some of the earliest references to this loyal, enthusiastic band appear, ironically, in connection with one of the biggest disasters of Bruckner's life: the première of the Third Symphony by the Vienna Philharmonic on 16 December 1877. Bruckner's champion Johann Herbeck had fought strong opposition to arrange the performance in the Musikverein, but on 28 October he died suddenly. Bruckner had to conduct the Symphony himself. The members of the orchestra appear to have been unco-operative from the start, and the symphony's effusive dedication to Wagner evidently prejudiced some members of the Viennese press before they had heard or seen a note of the work itself. Here are extracts from three reviews, beginning with the most notorious of them all.

EDUARD HANSLICK

The music critic Eduard Hanslick (1825–1904) was enormously influential in and beyond his own lifetime; his writings on music aesthetics are still valued in academic circles today. In his own field he could be very insightful; with anything beyond that field, however, he was curtly dismissive. Hanslick once wrote that, for him, music 'really begins with Mozart and culminates in Beethoven, Schumann and Brahms'. Earlier composers mattered little to him, and for Wagner and his followers he had nothing but scorn. This review appeared in the Vienna paper, *Neue Freie Presse*, two days after the first performance of Bruckner's Third Symphony. Hanslick's claim that he did 'not enjoy upsetting the composer' should be taken with more than a pinch of salt; during 1874–5 he had led a campaign to prevent Bruckner from attaining a lectureship at the University of Vienna.

The second concert in the Gesellschaft der Musikfreunde season was not put together very well. The programme was very long and the list of works was extensive: however, the audience did not derive an equivalently high degree of pleasure from it . . . The closing piece was a new symphony (No. 2 [*sic*!] in D minor) by Anton Bruckner, Court Organist and professor at the Conservatory. We do not enjoy upsetting the composer, whom we seriously respect as both a person and an artist, and who is certainly serious about art, however little he may have to do with it. For this reason, instead of criticizing him we would rather make the modest confession that we did not understand his gigantic symphony. His poetic intentions were not clear to us – perhaps a vision of how

Beethoven's Ninth befriends Wagner's *Walküre* and ends by being trampled under her horses' hoofs. Nor were we able to comprehend the purely musical coherence of the piece. The composer, who took on the conducting himself, was greeted with applause, and when the concert was over the small fraction of the audience that had stuck it out until the end clapped energetically in order to console him for the flight of the others.

[*Neue Freie Presse*, 18 December 1877 – reproduced in Göllerich/Auer, 4/1, 479]

WIENER ZEITUNG

The second concert in the winter series of the Gesellschaft der Musikfreunde took place yesterday. On the rostrum was Herr Joseph Hellmesberger, making his farewell appearance as temporary director of the Gesellschaft concerts . . . The final item was a gigantic symphony (in D minor) by Bruckner, who conducted the work in person. It is an enormous work, whose audacities and peculiarities cannot be characterized in a few words; so perhaps we may be permitted to dwell on it. An unrestrained and undisciplined naturalism* is at work in this baffling music, in which no crudity is too great, no logical leap too far, and which perpetrates the most outrageous acts with a truly childlike conviction. Herr Bruckner murders father and mother with the assurance that it has to be so. The things he achieves by means of the pause border on the fantastic. The listener constantly shakes his head, and from time to time even feels his pulse, to make sure that what he hears is not the product of his own feverish imaginings. Nevertheless, by virtue of its very definite claim to life, this delayed messenger from antediluvian times is of more lasting interest than many a well-ordered and virtuous symphony by a dry young scholar. Part of the audience left the hall even before Herr Bruckner had taken up his baton, and this exodus grew in scale after each of the movements. The finale, which surpasses all its predecessors in strangeness, was played to no more than a tiny band of determined daredevils. Far be it from us to defend this deplorable habit of the Vienna public.

*'Naturalism' is used here in a pejorative sense, meaning 'primitivism' or 'naïve instinctualism'.

[*Wiener Zeitung* (evening edition), 17 December 1877 – anonymous review]

DEUTSCHE ZEITUNG

Sunday's concert was a most enjoyable one, until Hellmesberger laid down his baton. Then came a new symphony by Anton Bruckner, directed by the composer himself. Many of the audience seem to have sensed something ominous in the air, and as time was getting on they headed for the exits. What followed showed how wise they had been. In the event we heard an utterly bizarre work, which might rather be described as a motley, formless patchwork fabricated from scraps of musical ideas than anything that is signified by the melodious title 'symphony'. The composer, who came to our attention when he gave a concert for the ending of the International Exhibition in 1873, is without doubt an original; but he must have either very few friends or none at all, because they would surely have prevented him from launching into such a farcical enterprise. The further the performance progressed, the more the Great Hall emptied. At the end a few jokers applauded loudly, calling out 'Bis' and 'Da capo'. As people left the hall complaints were heard: Herbeck was blamed for exposing musical Vienna to this regrettable experience, as it was he that had allowed the symphony to be performed. No doubt there is some truth in this, but one should not forget that Herr Bruckner is a professor at the Conservatory, and that Richard Wagner has accepted the dedication of this work. Under such circumstances did Herbeck have any right to intervene, and would that have achieved anything? The answer to these questions is a simple one: let the dead rest in peace!

[*Deutsche Zeitung*, 19 December 1877 – anonymous review. Both reviews published in *A German Reader, Music in the Making*, 133–6]

It seems the anonymous critic of the *Deutsche Zeitung* misinterpreted the intentions of what he calls the 'few jokers' who applauded at the end. But that very misunderstanding is probably a reflection of the dire mood towards the end of the concert. The next account of the Third Symphony's première is given by one of that tiny handful of Bruckner-supporters. Sympathetic as it is, it does not make happy reading.

THEODOR RÄTTIG

Theodor Rättig was the proprietor of the Bösendorfer publishing house, Büssjager & Rättig. His offer to publish the Third Symphony was, as he says, a timely gesture. Rättig published the orchestral score and a four-hand piano arrangement by Rudolf Krzyzanowksi and the seventeen-year-old Gustav Mahler, who had also attended the performance in the Musikverein and, like Rättig, had been deeply impressed by what he heard.

As a member of the Choral Society, I attended almost all the orchestral rehearsals. It was a pitiful and scandalous spectacle to see how the young players in the orchestra made fun of the old man's incompetent conducting. He had no real idea how to conduct properly and had to limit himself to giving the tempo and the style of a marionette. For this reason the composition itself seemed all the more impressive to me, and it awoke in me the conviction that one of the most powerful musical geniuses of all time was about to tread the thorny path which is customary, one is tempted to say prescribed, for such great individuals. The performance completely confirmed my opinion. A group of ten to twenty mainly very young people, both male and female, who stayed and applauded, stood in opposition to the hissing and laughing crowds. The oracles of the musical élite were sniggering: splendid entertainment for their dinner-tables at home. When the audience had left the hall and the musicians had cleared the platform, a small group of pupils and admirers gathered around the sorrowing Master, trying to comfort him, but he shouted, 'Oh, let me go, people don't want anything of mine.' Then I myself stepped into the circle; I expressed my admiration to the Master in the warmest terms, and offered to publish the work which had just been hissed off the platform. I explained that I would do so at my own cost (about 3,000 florins) and that I would give it the presentation it deserved. To the astonishment of the musical world, the work was published and this event probably gave the first positive stimulus to the wider appreciation of its creator. But great and naïve individuals are not grateful people, and there is probably nobody who made the lives of his warmest friends and admirers as difficult as did Anton Bruckner. When I gave him the beautifully engraved and bound first copy of the Third, he opened it, laughing joyfully, then suddenly burst out, 'For God's sake! It says here "Dedicated to the Master Rich. Wagner in deepest admiration", it should say "respect".' It was and remained very difficult to comfort him over this terrible mistake.

[Göllerich/Auer, 4/1, 477–8]

FREIDRICH ECKSTEIN

Friedrich Eckstein met Bruckner for the first time in autumn 1879, i.e. less than a year after the première of the Third Symphony. He now relates how he became a member of Bruckner's 'Gaudeamus'.

After that first meeting with Bruckner I often had the opportunity to meet the Master again and to exchange a few words with him: in the street, in cafés, in the concert hall and at the opera. But it wasn't until much later, in 1881, that I came into closer personal contact with him, through the friends of my youth, Schalk, Löwe and Hynais. Initially Bruckner's pupils, they soon became the chief proclaimers of his genius. Once, during an oratorio concert, we were all together in the standing-part of the hall, when Bruckner came and joined us, and after some lively debating on the way home it was finally decided that we should all go to a nearby inn for dinner. Like Hugo Wolf, Gustav Mahler and other musicians of that time, Bruckner listened to concerts from the standing-area, and it always gave us food for thought when we saw Johannes Brahms above, enthroned in solitary splendour, in the normally unapproachable Director's Box.

Our time together in the restaurant made a very pleasant harmonious conclusion to a fine evening. Right from the start, Bruckner's behaviour towards me was very cordial, and I took it as a special honour when he invited me to spend another evening with him soon. In time this became an institution, and for years I spent all my free evenings in the circle of Bruckner and his favourite pupils. Bruckner gave me the affectionate nickname 'Samiel', because my 'wild' hairstyle reminded him of the Prince of Darkness in Weber's *Freischütz*. Josef Schalk on the other hand was known as the 'Generalissimus', because of the high standing he enjoyed amongst us.

[Eckstein, 138–9]

ERNST DECSEY

Another of Bruckner's pupils, Ernst Decsey, now gives his account of the Bruckner circle. How much of this is based on personal memory and how much on hindsight is not always easy to tell. Decsey's first encounter with Bruckner himself did not take place until 1889; but the general ethos of 'Gaudeamus' and of the Viennese 'Academic Wagner Society' was evidently well known to him. While allowing certain criticisms of Löwe, Josef Schalk and the 'Bruckner Party' in general, his final verdict is essentially positive.

Two young artists were especially active on Bruckner's behalf. One of these was his pupil Ferdinand Löwe, the other his friend Josef Schalk. Born in Vienna in 1865, Löwe made his first public appearance as a nine-year-old pianistic prodigy. Ten years later, in 1884, at his first fully independent concert the young lion* showed his claws: amongst other things he played his own piano arrangement of the Adagio from Bruckner's Linz Symphony [No. 2], which caused quite a stir. 'The arrangement, completely faithful to the score yet eminently pianistic, revealed an altogether exceptional talent for this interpretative art' (Theodor Helm: *Memoirs*). Löwe continued to advance in this direction. He became professor of piano at the Conservatory, then an orchestral conductor in Pest, Munich and Vienna, eventually finding a permanent position at the Konzertverein, founded in 1901. Wherever he went, he took with him something by Bruckner. His well-balanced nature, his extraordinary innate musicality, which together with his non-

*The name Löwe means 'lion'.

partisan attitude particularly suited him to be the musical representative of Vienna – he is now director of the Musikakademie – his broad gesture, his calm strength, all this of made him a born Bruckner conductor.

Josef Schalk, born in 1857, the elder of the two, was an altogether quieter type. Always somewhat sickly – he died prematurely in 1900 at Gossensass – he guarded his devotion and conviction like sacred flames. In 1887 he was appointed successor to Schütt (who in 1885 had performed the *Te Deum* at the piano) as leader of the Wagner Society, where he dedicated himself to fostering the 'rising generation': Anton Bruckner, then Hugo Wolf. This dedication often brought him close to exhaustion. He acted as Bruckner's piano-arranger, alone or with Löwe, and by dubbing him 'Generalissimus', Bruckner showed what he thought of him. With his brother Franz he made amongst other things the first piano arrangement of the Seventh Symphony, a courageous act at that time, as much for the publisher as for the young musicians, who moved outside the favoured circle. In October 1884 Schalk's first article on Bruckner appeared in the Bayreuth papers, a pure labour of love. It seems that the age brought forth men who were loyal and self-denying, as if nature wished to lend strength to the great man in his helplessness. It came in the form of these three Brucknerites: Löwe, Josef and Franz Schalk.

Besides the relatively few official Bruckner performances at the Philharmonic, there were always the Bruckner Party's piano and orchestral concerts, which gained the composer much new ground. Everywhere the campaigners took up the fight, everywhere there were skirmishes, little assaults, great battles, first at Bösendorfer's, then in the Musikvereinsaal or the Prater. First the Wagnerverein won over Hans Richter, and entrusted him with a performance of the *Romantic* Symphony (29 January 1888), then Schalk overcame his shyness and gave the same symphony in the Theatre and Music Exhibition (15 June 1892), and finally there were guest appearances in Munich, Graz, Prague and Pest. 'Wagner Society' was becoming synonymous with 'Bruckner Society'. A revolution was in progress.

It was often claimed that Bruckner was unduly swayed by his apostles, or, in other words, that he had become the pupil of his pupils. In particular, it was alleged that Josef Schalk had imposed his will on the often doubt-ridden composer, that he was in fact responsible for the pianissimo conclusion of the first movement of the Eighth Symphony, to name but one example. It was believed precisely because it was absurd. The only element of truth in the legend is that the actual writing out of a modern full orchestral score was sometimes too much for Bruckner, whose music was always painstakingly, never quickly composed. He needed help in the mechanical process, like the medieval Masters who entrusted the more menial aspects of the execution to journeymen and apprentices. And since his 'journeymen' were not automata but young intellectuals, they felt compelled to make practical suggestions, and the Master, perhaps seeing his own scruples reflected in them, would give in on smaller matters.

At any rate, Schalk and Löwe behaved honestly and selflessly, with a sense of their responsibility as apostles. That in such a relationship there should sometimes be misunderstandings, angry or strained moments, is only natural, and it gives Carl Hruby no right to indulge in coarse attacks on the 'two great panjandrums'.*

[Ernst Decsey, *Bruckner, Versuch eines Lebens*, Berlin, 1920, 100–102]

CARL HRUBY

The particular 'coarse attack' quoted by Ernst Decsey occurs in the following extract from Carl Hruby's *Meine Erinnerungen an Anton Bruckner.* Hruby paints a very different picture of the Bruckner circle, especially of the brothers Schalk.

Bruckner's affability and his generally open nature also made it possible for undesirable elements to worm their way into his company, people intent on basking in his glory. Tiresome though this kind of person could be, he was too weak and good-natured to be constantly shaking them off. For this reason, his true friends and admirers were often kept away, from time to time actually driven off. (The above-mentioned characteristic may have contributed to this: 'Try not to offend anyone, as you never know from

*'Two great panjandrums': Hruby's splendid original is *die beiden Oberbonzen.*

which quarter harm might come.') To this category – those for whom he had no real liking but was still afraid to offend – belonged the two great panjandrums of Vienna Academic Wagner Society, who (at first very much against his will!) appointed themselves his apostles, purely to further their own interests. 'There's no one else who'll stand up for me,' he explained, resignedly. The first of these two gentlemen suffered occasional fits of poesy, which he then inflicted on musical works (to make them more accessible!) in the form of literary interpretations. 'Programmes' was how he described these strange products of a poetry-diseased brain. Unfortunately it was invariably Bruckner's symphonies that he chose as the playground for his quixotic literary adventures. The wonderful, fresh, quintessentially Brucknerian Scherzo of the Seventh Symphony, in which the Master's sense of humour rose to unsuspected heights, conjured up this: 'the ethereal vaults of heaven, in which good spirits perform a blissful round-dance' (!!!). One can imagine the relish with which the anti-Brucknerian press fell upon this fatuous nonsense. For them, as the Viennese say, it was '*ein gefundenes Treffen*' – 'fair game'. Their reviews were as good as written: the programme was just as muddled as the symphony itself! Bruckner was incensed. 'Why's he picked on my Seventh for his poetry?' he exclaimed in the height of his anger; 'The arsehole knows exactly what I was thinking about – at most, the few hundred guilders I might get out of a publisher!' But these chronic poetic fits were beyond the reach of medicine, and on the occasion of the first performance of the Master's Eighth Symphony the world was once again blessed with the arrival of a 'programme', one which put all previous efforts in the shade. How little Bruckner trusted the friendship of the two above-named gentlemen can be illustrated with the following choice morsel. One of them had borrowed the original score of the Seventh Symphony and Bruckner was keen to rescue it, but despite repeated reminders it was not returned. When all else had failed, Bruckner finally sent Kathi, adding that she might like to 'say something' to the gentleman. And nobody could 'say something' like Kathi! Having done just that, Kathi returned with the score safe and sound. 'I snatched it off him,' she reported proudly. Bruckner always laughed when he talked about Kathi's triumph. And now comes something very interesting! Bruckner claimed to have found an alteration in one of the trumpet parts! He was sure that he had written it quite differently! Of course it was not true, but it shows well how deeply mistrustful Bruckner could be on certain occasions.

In contrast there were his true friends, those of whom he was genuinely fond. These included the already-mentioned Grossauer, who had grown up in the same region as Bruckner, and another Upper Austrian, by name Almeroth, who once came all the way from Milan to Vienna solely to be present at a performance of the Quintet. Then there was his former pupil August Göllerich, and the Landgraf Vinzenz Fürstenburg. Nor should one forget Schenner, Professor of Piano at the Conservatory, nor the honest but often somewhat voluble Dr Theodor Helm, who was the first Vienna critic to stand up for Bruckner. (The writer of these lines also enjoyed Bruckner's special favour.) A further supporter was the brilliant Hugo Wolf, who throughout his life remained a true, sincere admirer of Bruckner. Hugo Wolf was perhaps the only composer of the new generation – Mahler and R[ichard] Strauss were still virtually unknown at that time – whom Bruckner took seriously and recognized and admired without qualification. He described the declamation in Wolf's *Lieder und Gesänge* as little short of genius! 'That fellow can spend his whole day just composing, while I have to torture myself teaching . . .' he said, in a fit of comical jealousy. While Wolf – at least in latter times – was able to compose undisturbed, Bruckner was compelled to give lessons – at three guilders an hour – even when he was in his sixties, in order to make an income and thus to create a comfortable life for himself.

[Hruby, 16–19]

The next anecdote, reported by Alma Mahler in *Erinnerungen und Briefe*, tends to confirm Hruby's portrayal of the Bruckner–Brothers Schalk relationship.

ALMA MAHLER

Bruckner had two pupils who made all the piano arrangements of his symphonies, but who seem to have bullied and tormented him. They were the brothers Schalk. Bruckner was very fond of Mahler and entrusted him with the piano arrangement of his Third Symphony. When Mahler brought him the newly prepared first movement, Bruckner was full of naïve delight and said with a mischievous smile, 'Now I don't need the Schalks any more!' This saying became a household word with us and it was quoted at every possible (and impossible) opportunity.

[Alma Mahler, 132]

FRANZ AND JOSEF SCHALK

Not surprisingly, neither Franz (1863–1931) nor Josef (1857–1901) Schalk describes relations with Bruckner in quite the same terms as Alma Mahler or Carl Hruby; but every now and again there are illuminating remarks. In 1881, Franz Schalk persuaded the conductor of the Karslrühe Philharmonic Society, Felix Mottl, to perform the Third Symphony (eighteen-year-old Franz was then serving as a violinist in Mottl's orchestra). All that was necessary was for Josef to obtain Bruckner's permission. If Hruby and Mahler's allegations are accepted, then Bruckner's mistrustfulness is less than surprising.

I am astonished that Bruckner will not let the symphony out of his hands, because at first he trusted me with it, and I was well aware of the responsibility. You can tell him that the performance is arranged for 14 December. Perhaps that will persuade him.

[Franz to Josef Schalk, 1 November 1881]

Compare the next letter, from Josef to Franz Schalk, with Carl Hruby's story about Bruckner, Josef Schalk and the score of the Seventh Symphony (pp. 120–1). Fortunately for posterity, Bruckner never seriously revised the Seventh, but there is one controversial detail:

the cymbal clash, with timpani and triangle, at the climax of the Adagio (figure W). Over these percussion parts, somebody (almost certainly not Bruckner) has written *gilt nicht* ('not valid'). This letter makes it clear whom we have to thank for them.

Löwe and I have recently gone through the score of the Seventh with Bruckner, discussing one or two alterations and improvements. You probably don't know that Nikisch has got him to agree to our cymbal-clash in the Adagio (C major 6–4 chord), along with the triangle and the timpani – to our unbounded delight.

[Josef to Franz Schalk – Vienna, 10 January 1885]
[Franz Schalk, *Briefe und Betrachtungen*, published by Lili Schalk, 36, 49]

There is a widespread notion that Bruckner invariably gave in meekly to pressure from the Schalks. But the idea that Bruckner never put up a fight is vividly contradicted by the next reminiscence. Friedrich Klose attended the rehearsals for Josef Schalk's and Franz Zottman's 1887 performance of their two-piano arrangement of the Fifth Symphony, and heard the concert itself. This is his report.

FRIEDRICH KLOSE

Josef Schalk and Zottmann wanted to surprise Bruckner with a public performance of his Fifth Symphony in the original arrangement for two pianos, and so they prepared it in secret. At that time the Master was in bad spirits. In my diary – obviously brimming over with youthful fury – I describe Bruckner's behaviour towards his friends as 'crazy', 'uncouth', and 'outrageous'. This mood of his must have been the reason why, when Schalk invited him to the above-mentioned event, hoping that it would give him pleasure, Bruckner got into a rage and declared he should have asked his permission first; and as this had not happened, he was forbidding the performance.

Now followed a scene that I shall never forget. It happened at Gause's Restaurant, in the large dining-hall. Bruckner and Schalk sat on the long side of the table, opposite each other. Adalbert von

Goldschmidt and I sat at the ends. Schalk explained that he and Zottmann had carefully prepared the work, and that they had believed they were respecting the composer's intentions, but Bruckner replied that he had to be convinced of that first. In that case, said Schalk, the final rehearsal was the ideal opportunity. The final rehearsal would be too late, said Bruckner resolutely; it should have happened during the preparation, since his wishes as to the performance of this very difficult work could not possibly be implemented at the last minute. The concert must be postponed, and the necessary rehearsals should be carried out under his direction.

SCHALK Changing the date's out of the question. The poster is already with the printer; and as to whether we can get the Bösendorfersaal on another evening, that's debatable to say the least.

BRUCKNER (*obstinately*) All right then, the concert's off!

SCHALK (*angrily, in a low voice*) You can't possibly mean that, Herr Professor, not after all the money that's been spent on it – it would all be lost if we had to cancel!

BRUCKNER (*bent forward over the table, shaking with rage*) I order you!

SCHALK (*also bent forward, hissing*) The concert goes ahead!

BRUCKNER (*in a strangled voice, rapping on the table with his knuckles*) In that case, Herr Schalk, I'll call the police!

The two adversaries set on each other like fighting cockerels, quite oblivious of Goldschmidt and myself, for whom it made a priceless spectacle. After this dramatic climax, the fury abated, the combatants grew gradually calmer, and when Schalk consented to the moving of the concert and promised as many extra rehearsals as Bruckner required, a truce was declared.

But it was only a truce; during the rehearsals the fighting broke out again. The following entries in my diary say all that needs to be said:

4 April 1887. Rehearsal of the Fifth Symphony. Bruckner treats Schalk and Zottmann like slaves, 4.00, second rehearsal. Again, relentless ill-treatment.

5 April. 10.30, rehearsal at the Bösendorfer. Bruckner wants three more

rehearsals. Zottman and Schalk unwilling – especially Schalk, who's already quite ill. So the concert is off again. Finally it is agreed to move the date again.

14 April. Rehearsal of the Fifth. Bruckner's temper flares up again.

15 April. Rehearsal. Bruckner unbearable.

16 April. Bruckner demands the impossible. Schalk resists him vigorously.

I can still clearly remember these unpleasant scenes. Offended that no one had sought his permission for this event, Bruckner had resolved, with the obstinacy of an Upper-Austrian *Mostschädel** to find fault with everything, simply to make the point that, without him, performance of the work as he conceived it was impossible. He sat in the front row, the score on his knee, and interrupted continually, complaining that a thematic inner part wasn't strong enough, or that he couldn't hear this or that figuration, the next minute declaring that no one could make out the contrapuntal lines when the playing was so ill-defined; and then the forte passages weren't loud enough, even though the players were at the end of their strength and their fingers were almost bleeding from the effort. None of this bothered Bruckner in the slightest; everything had to be repeated, and then he would direct his malicious remarks mainly at poor Schalk, the ringleader of this criminal conspiracy to put on an unauthorized concert, and therefore the chief scapegoat. For example, if Bruckner asked which of the two gentlemen had the melody in the inversion, and it turned out to be Zottmann, then the Master was content merely to ask for greater clarity; but if the detail in question lay in the other part, then out came the barbed remarks: 'Herr Schalk is always so delicate, protecting the public's nerves', or: 'the Herr Generalissimus plays so spiritually that one can hardly hear him.' One can understand why in the end Schalk protested vigorously at this behaviour, particularly as the objections were less objective points than mere chicanery, as I could see, sitting beside Bruckner and looking with him at the score. He wanted to hear each part of the contrapuntal texture clearly, and one can imagine the result of his insistence: a

**Mostschädel*, a 'wine-skull' – an inverate drunkard . . .

pounding on the groaning pianos by the two players that lacked any clear shading, a meaningless noise, like a caricature of the original orchestral sound-picture. Naturally Bruckner was himself dissatisfied with this and demanded more rehearsals. This time, however, Schalk and Zottmann were adamant, and so the concert took place, at last, on 20 April 1887.

Bruckner sat in the back row of the Bösendorfersaal, surrounded by his friends. He was in a very irritable mood; enquiries were not answered. His head moved nervously back and forth – as I have said, this was always a sign of strained nerves in the Master. During the performance of the symphony he sat like a tiger, waiting for the moment to pounce. The determination to find the performance wanting was obvious. As soon as the last note had been sounded a great cheer went up. The performers indicated the composer. Everyone turned towards him. But Bruckner did not move, only looked about angrily. We wanted to show him to the wildly applauding audience, but he brushed us off roughly. Suddenly his expression lit up, as though he had been touched by a magic wand. Springing up from his seat, he darted through the raging sea of people, stood before them and, with his hands crossed over his chest, his expression radiant, he bowed again and again. Then 'all's well that ends well'; after the concert came a little celebration at Gause's, where cheerfulness reigned and, according to my diary, the contented Master 'treated everyone to the best wine'.

[Klose, 140–44]

SIGISMUND BACHRICH

In 1869, the year after Bruckner's move to Vienna, Sigismund Bachrich (1841–1913) became Professor of Violin at the Vienna Conservatory and lead viola player in the Vienna Philharmonic; he was to remain with the orchestra for thirty years, taking part in several Bruckner performances, possibly including the première of the Third Symphony in 1877. He was a member of the Hellmesberger Quartet, and later of the Rosé Quartet. According to Max Auer, Bachrich was originally one of Bruckner's most prominent detractors –

> though Bachrich himself fails to mention this in his memoirs. He recalls Bruckner in his more successful, later years. By then, the number of passionate Bruckner enthusiasts had grown from a handful of students to what Ernst Decsey termed a fully fledged 'Party'. Decsey's use of that word implies a political dimension, which Bachrich now confirms.

At the performance of a new work by Brahms one could hear how powerfully the Protestant community supported him, while Bruckner reaped the thunderous applause of the so-called Christian Social Party. I am not suggesting that religious politics had crept into the concert hall, but the possibility that one party would exalt its figurehead to spite the other could not be discounted. After the last chord of a newly performed work, the audience would show by its determined applause how urgent was its desire to see the composer appear on the podium. This much achieved, his followers took care of the rest. With Brahms, this was no simple matter. He listened to his new work hidden away in a corner of the hall, and before the end he would creep away softly. Only the alertness of the Philharmonic staff prevented him from leaving, and Richter would have to seize him and convey him with gentle force onto the podium. With Goldmark, things ran more smoothly, though even he would dally a fair while before making his appearance. Only good old Bruckner was always ready at his post. No sooner had the din started than he was there, thanking them in his child-like, naïve way, and this was repeated endlessly. Bruckner's followers would still be cheering him long after we musicians had packed our instruments away.

[Bachrich, *Aus veklungenen Zeiten, Erinnerungen eines alten Musikers*, Vienna, 1914, 99–101]

The Honourable Israelites

Sigismund Bachrich's cautiousness on the subject of 'religious politics' is more understandable if one considers the political scene in Vienna in the last decade and a half of the nineteenth century. The Austrian Christian Social Party (*Christlichsoziale Partei*) was founded in 1887 under the leadership of Karl Lueger (1844–1910), later Mayor of Vienna; Lueger has the distinction of having been a formative influence on the politics and leadership style of Adolf Hitler. Under Lueger's leadership, the Christian Social Party claimed to stand for the 'little man', and against powerful entrepreneurs and financiers; it made no secret of its anti-Semitism.

Was Bruckner a sympathizer, or was he merely, 'naïvely', glad of any powerful support in Vienna? A strict, monastery-educated Catholic in nineteenth-century Austria could be expected to have deeply conservative views on the monarchy, 'family values' and such like, and as a Catholic he would almost certainly have been taught that the Jews were collectively guilty of the murder of Christ. But accounts of Bruckner's attitude to the Jews are contradictory. Bruckner was more than tolerant towards Jewish friends and supporters: he addressed the conductor Hermann Levi as *mein künstlerischer Vater* ('my artistic father'), and he seems to have had genuine affection and respect for Mahler – though Marie Lorenz, sister-in-law of Rudolf Krzyzanowski, told August Göllerich that Bruckner was 'disturbed' by Mahler's Jewishness (Göllerich/Auer, 4/1, 532). Friedrich Eckstein relates how Bruckner was once 'deeply moved' by Jewish burial rites and songs ('*Alte unnennbare Tage!*', 169), although, confusingly, he mentions this in the middle of an account of Hans Rott's funeral – Rott was not Jewish. The next three stories suggest that Bruckner's feelings on the subject of the Jews were far from consistent.

ALMA MAHLER

In those early days Mahler would often go with Bruckner to the tavern for lunch. Bruckner paid for the beer while Mahler had to see to the rolls, and as Mahler had no money at that time, lunch often went by the way. Bruckner was always surrounded by a large circle of young musicians, to whom he spoke with childlike unrestraint. But if there were Jews in the company he would always refer politely to 'the Honourable Israelites' if he had anything to say on that subject.

[Alma Mahler, 132]

MAX VON OBERLEITHNER

Herr Almeroth, a friend of Bruckner from Steyr, told me the following little story. The painter Uhde* saw Bruckner at a gathering in Munich and asked Almeroth if he could arrange a sitting with Bruckner. When Almeroth informed Bruckner that a famous painter wanted to use his striking head as a model for an apostle at the Last Supper, Bruckner replied, 'But I'm no Jew!' and then, 'Nor am I worthy to pose as an apostle at the Last Supper!'

Bruckner let the word 'Jew' slip from his mouth only because of his extreme excitement; otherwise he hardly ever used it. He preferred to say, 'the honourable Israelites'.

[Oberleithner, 75]

JOHANN KERSCHAGL

Johann Nepomuk Kerschagl attended Bruckner's lectures at the Vienna Conservatory; he later became a schoolteacher. Introducing Kerschagl's reminiscence, August Göllerich writes that 'Bruckner's aversion to the Jews differed from the indiscriminate hatred of the anti-Semites. As a result of his sincere and deeply held religious faith, he transformed these feelings into deep

*Fritz von Uhde (1848–1911), German painter. His paintings of scenes from the New Testament were, in their time, highly controversial.

sympathy.' Whatever one thinks of Göllerich's distinction, the following story does not suggest a profound racist hatred.

Once, the Master walked into a classroom during a harmony lesson at the Conservatory, greeting the mass of pupils with his usual warm openness. Then his eye fixed on a small Jewish boy (he later became a member of an important Viennese orchestra),* who was sitting in the front row – an unprepossessing figure who looked younger than he actually was. Bruckner went over to him, looked at him for a while and then placed a hand on his curly-haired Jewish head and said, with something close to compassion, 'Dear child, do you really believe that the Messiah has not yet come to Earth?' The youngsters in the classroom almost burst with laughter, but Bruckner, the devout Catholic, meant it in all seriousness!

[From Göllerich/Auer, 4/1, 532–3]

*According to Göllerich, the boy was Josef Laser, later a cellist in the Vienna Concert Society.

The Master of all Masters

Several of the writers included in this book refer to Bruckner as *der Meister*. 'The Master' is the inevitable English translation, though it misses something of the German term's associations with medieval mastercraftsmanship, a concept with religious–nationalist overtones for some German-speaking romantics. The idea is embodied in the final chorus of Wagner's *Die Meistersinger*: 'Ehrt eure deutschen Meister' ('honour your German Masters').

For Bruckner, Wagner was the only living human being to be referred to as 'Master'. His reverence for Wagner the composer bordered on the idolatrous. True, there is little evidence that he was influenced by Wagner's philosophical, political or aesthetic thinking. Nevertheless, the meeting with Wagner in September 1873 was evidently one of the great events of Bruckner's life. Bruckner took with him his two most recent symphonies, No. 2 in C minor and No. 3 in D minor, in the hope that Wagner might accept the dedication of one of them. Three versions of this meeting follow: the first two are recollections of how Bruckner himself described it; the third is an eye-witness account. Unfortunately, Wagner's own thoughts on this extraordinary encounter do not appear to have been recorded.

AUGUST GÖLLERICH

He often recalled this day, the happiest of his life, in conversation with people from his homeland, describing the events in his friendly, informal manner: 'I was utterly overwhelmed by the splendour of Wahnfried. I didn't know where to put my feet on the carpet.' Standing in the hall, he heard the Master playing. 'Then I acted like a schoolboy – I peeped through the keyhole, but I couldn't see a thing since the piano was in the other corner.' Eventually Wagner appeared and Bruckner made to kiss his hand. Bruckner stammered something about dedicating a symphony.

Wagner replied, somewhat curtly, 'As if I wasn't swamped by things like this already. Come back in three days.' Bruckner was in agony: 'In three days I'll have no money left, it won't last that long,' he thought. But he dared not argue; instead he said, remorsefully, 'Master, I know I don't have the right to rob you of your precious time, I just thought that by quickly looking at the themes the Master would know what was what.' 'Well, come in then,' Wagner said with a smile, and led him into the drawing-room.

'As the Master leafed through the scores, I felt like a schoolboy whose book's being corrected by the teacher, and took every "look, look!" to be a black mark. But since I'd already begun to ask, I kept on stammering about the dedication. I explained that it was the one and only, the greatest honour I'd ever desired! "I don't allow anything to be dedicated to me that I haven't seen," said Wagner, and I was told to leave the score there.'

In the afternoon Bruckner went up to the site where the Festspielhaus was being built. There he mingled with the excavators and bricklayers who talked to him affably about the Master, all of which warmed his heart. Despite the rain, he clambered around looking at everything and tirelessly asking questions until, rather unexpectedly, he fell backwards into a fortunately empty mortar trough.

At this point, a servant from Wahnfried suddenly appeared, having looked for Bruckner for some time, to inform him that the Master requested his presence immediately! The workmen then had to give him a quick makeshift rub-down. Hardly giving them time to do this, he shouted, 'Clean me up lads, I beg you, clean me up – I've got to see the Master!

'When I arrived at Wahnfried, Cosima was waiting in the hall. I kissed her hand and said, "Surely I owe this good fortune to a word you put in for me with your husband?" "Oh no!" she replied. "As far as music's concerned I've got no influence over him. He won't have any interfering on that front. Go to the Master. He asked for you himself." '

As he stepped into the next room, he heard the Master at the piano, playing the main theme of the first movement of the Third Symphony himself; in fact, while he was standing in the hall he heard Wagner flick back through the score twice and play it three times – 'My theme, imagine that!' As the Master stopped, Bruckner knocked shyly at the door. 'I knocked once, twice, and finally got an indignant "Come in!" ' On entering the room, Bruckner saw that Wagner was still standing at the piano, holding the score. But Wagner stepped towards him, the score in his left hand, stretching the right out to him.

'First of all, he said nothing, just looked at me with such a kind gaze that I can still feel it today. Then he embraced me and kissed me again and again. Afterwards he pointed to a pile of music and said, "Look – nothing but dedications. But your work is a masterpiece; I am pleased and honoured that it's intended for me." The Master said that to me! Imagine that!!

'Of course I had to cry straight away, and it didn't get any better when he finally accepted the dedication!

'We then sat down together with the score of the D minor Symphony and straight away he picked out the main points, sang and whistled the themes, and every other minute he gave a loud "Bravo!" and patted me on the back so hard that it would have hurt if it hadn't been meant so kindly!

'Afterwards I stayed with him till eight o'clock. The Master had a keg of beer brought to him, and with the first glass he said to me, "And now dear friend, let's drink to your work." ' In doing so, Wagner himself took a glass over to Bruckner, who said, 'But Master, such a waiter!' Eva Wagner, still a very young girl, was also there. Bruckner often liked to tell people how he played with Eva, who smiled at him, and how Wagner jokingly called her Bruckner's bride.

'Later I admired all the beautiful pictures of Wagner that were hung around the room. The Master said, "I much prefer the portrait of my wife to the ones of me!" Then we talked a lot about the musical situation in Vienna and Wagner grew very angry about the conditions at the Court Opera Theatre, which he called "rough". I defended Herbeck, though it was no use. Then the Master really laid into Hanslick, who soon afterwards was to become my executioner.'

The following day Bruckner was beset by doubt as to which of the two symphonies Wagner had accepted. He was beside himself about it, and in the end he sent someone, as early as possible, to ask Wagner. He wrote him a note on a sheet of blue writing paper in the hotel, marked, 'W. Köhler, Zum goldenen Anker, Bayreuth', on which he wrote, 'Symphony in D minor, where the trumpet begins the theme? A. Bruckner.' Soon afterwards, the servant returned with the note, on which Wagner had replied to Bruckner's question with the words, 'Yes, yes! Very best wishes! Richard Wagner.'

[Göllenrich/Auer, 4/1, 232–6]

MAX VON OBERLEITHNER

In 1873 Bruckner went to Marienbad for the cure. From there, he wrote to Wagner at Bayreuth, saying that unless he received anything to the contrary, he would take the liberty to call on the Master. There was no such reply, and so one morning Bruckner knocked at Wagner's door. It turned out that the Master was not free at that moment, and Bruckner was told to come back at five o'clock. 'Alas,' Bruckner sighed, but then came a servant with a new instruction: he should come back at twelve o'clock. At twelve precisely he presented himself. 'Come in, Bruckner,' said the Master, and when Bruckner asked if he would look at his compositions, Wagner showed him the piles of documents relating to the Festspielhaus and pointed out that for six weeks he had not been able to work on the *Nibelungen*.

Undeterred, Bruckner said, 'Master, I am sure that for you just a look at the themes would be enough.' At this Wagner led him into the next room, leafed through the score of the Second Symphony and said, 'Very good.' But when he turned to the Third Symphony and saw the canon and the trumpet theme he stopped short and read through the whole of the first section carefully. Now Bruckner ventured a request: might he dedicate one of his symphonies to the Master? Wagner said, 'Leave me the score of the Third and come back at five o'clock.'

When Bruckner returned that afternoon he was met with a warm embrace and the words, 'As to the dedication, the answer is, yes. It would give me great pleasure.' In his joy Bruckner kissed Wagner's little daughter Eva. Wagner himself poured him a beer, and they sat together until half-past seven, lamenting the situation in Vienna.

[Oberleithner, 76–7]

GUSTAV KIETZ

Gustav Adolf Kietz (1824–1908) was a German sculptor who made several images of Wagner and eventually became a close friend. The bust of Cosima Wagner he refers below to was exhibited in the Villa Wahnfried after Wagner's death. Kietz's reminiscences of the composer were recorded by his wife, Marie, and published as *Richard Wagner in den Jahren 1842–1849 und 1873–1875*. His account of Wagner's and Bruckner's evening conversation, and of Bruckner's anxiety the following morning, is contained in a letter to Marie Kietz. It shows that the famous note on blue paper (see above p. 134) was by no means Bruckner's only attempt to find out which symphony he had dedicated to Wagner.

Yesterday afternoon, while I was alone at my work (the bust of Cosima), Wagner's servant brought in a small barrel of beer and set it down. 'What's that for?' I asked. 'There's a visitor,' he replied. Not long afterwards, in came Wagner, his wife and a little gentleman, whom Wagner introduced as Herr Anton Bruckner, a composer from Vienna. Although the following conversation was very lively I didn't pay much attention to it as I was preoccupied with my bust, for which Frau Cosima was posing. I heard only that music was the subject, that the strange gentleman wanted to talk about the enthusiasm of the Viennese for *Lohengrin*, and that Wagner kept stopping him, saying 'Oh, enough of that, I know all about that, a swan comes on with a knight, the same old stuff – here, have a drink instead. This is splendid stuff, Weihen-Stephan,' and Wagner handed him a huge, brimming glass with the words: 'Your health!' 'Oh, Master, for heaven's sake, I can't possibly, it would be the death of me! I've just come from Karlsbad!' 'Come now,' cried Wagner, 'this will do you good. Drink!' And again he filled the glass to the top, and the good Bruckner drank and drank, despite the wails and protests that comically punctuated his musical conversation. 'There's a true child of Vienna for you,' said Frau Cosima with a smile.

Early next morning, I was having my breakfast in the guest room of my hotel, when in came Anton Bruckner. As soon as he set eyes on me, he rushed at me with the words: 'Oh, Herr Hofrat, what luck that I've seen you – I'm the unluckiest man alive! You heard yesterday that I'd sent the Master some symphonies to select one for a dedication, and now I'm in a frightful position – I can't remember which one the Master chose. Oh, that beer, that terrible beer!' 'All I can remember', I replied, 'was something about a symphony in D minor, and then there was something else about a trumpet.' Once again, the true child of Vienna came to the fore. Bruckner embraced me passionately, kissed me on the cheeks, and cried: 'Oh, Herr Hofrat, my dear Hofrat' (how I came by this title I still don't know), 'How I can I ever thank you! Yes – it was the D minor which the Master accepted. Oh, if you knew the sensation it will cause in Vienna, when those gentlemen hear that the Master has accepted the dedication of a symphony from me!'

[Kietz, *Richard Wagner in den Jahren 1842–49 und 1873–75, Erinnerungen*, Dresden, 1905, 183–4]

CARL HRUBY

Carl Hruby summarizes more of Bruckner's recollections of his days at Bayreuth, including another version of the Eva Wagner story.

The times Bruckner spent at Bayreuth in the intimate company of his adored 'Master' were perhaps the happiest of his entire life. His eyes shone strangely whenever he came to speak of them. There are innumerable anecdotes on this subject in circulation, and I shall not bother to test their authenticity; I do not consider it my task to chew over them again. I will simply limit myself to a few unknown reminiscences which I myself heard from Bruckner's own mouth and whose truthfulness I can guarantee. They illustrate

Bruckner's childlike naïvety so well that I could not possibly keep them to myself.

For example, Bruckner related again and again, as if recalling one of his happiest memories, how on his frequent morning visits to the Villa 'Wahnfried', the 'Master of the Nibelungen' would come towards him, leading his little daughter Eva by the hand, and how he would lift up the 'radiant child of Wotan' and hand her over with the comic-serious words: 'Here, Bruckner, your bride!' The only problem for our composer was his inability to get on with Bülow, who never stopped 'ribbing' him, to use Bruckner's earthy description. There seems to have been a peculiar antipathy between those two great spirits. Certainly it is hard to imagine a sharper contrast than between Bruckner's childlike manner and the biting sarcasm of Herr von Bülow . . .*

One evening, Wagner invited Bruckner over to Wahnfried. Bruckner found the Master in the library, standing by the window, absorbed in a book. Wagner was in a melancholy, almost sombre mood. In the course of the conversation, when Bruckner had yet again given vent to his enthusiasm for the great composer in his typically unaffected and honest way, Wagner suddenly turned to him, fixed him with his soulful Wotan-like stare and asked: 'Do you really think so much of me, Bruckner?' Then Bruckner sank down on one knee, and returning that gaze with profound feeling, answered, 'Oh Master, I worship you!'** This was the only man before whom he had ever knelt, Bruckner later said. What he worshipped was purely the divine element that was revealed to the world in the human form of Richard Wagner. And one can understand this veneration bordering on idolatry: the eternal laurel adorning his own ageing head had blossomed forth from Wagner, or (in the Adagio of the Seventh Symphony) from Wagner's grave.

[Hruby, 34–5]

*An example of Hans von Bülow's 'biting sarcasm' was quoted by Brahms to Richard Heuberger. Apparently von Bülow said that if Bruckner ever wrote a Ninth Symphony, it should be called *Ode an die Schadenfreude* (The title of the Schiller poem set by Beethoven in his Ninth Symphony is *Ode an die Freude*, 'Ode to Joy'). (Heuberger: *Erinnerungen an Johannes Brahms*, 58)

**Bruckner relates this story himself in a letter to Hans von Wolzogen, but adds Wagner's response, 'Be calm, Bruckner. Goodnight!'

JOSEF WÖSS

The Austrian composer, editor and church musician Josef Wöss (1863–1943) studied at the Vienna Conservatory from 1880 to 1882, though not with Bruckner. After a career as a singing teacher and choral conductor, he joined the Vienna publishing house Universal Edition, where he was editor from 1908 to 1931, overseeing the publication of several scores by Bruckner; unfortunately these are full of the kind of distortions one finds in the so-called Schalk and Löwe 'editions'. Wöss's version of the Fourth Symphony remained in print (Eulenberg) until the 1980s, and its influence can be detected even in certain relatively recent recordings.

In Bayreuth at that time you could see splendid complete performances of *Parsifal*, *Tristan* and *Die Meistersinger*. After *Parsifal* I noticed that Bruckner's eyes were moist; it was the same after *Tristan*. After *Die Meistersinger*, however, he was laughing all over his face, and during the supper that followed he was in an extremely cheerful, almost boisterous mood. We went to see *Parsifal* again. Once the performance was over, Bruckner gathered us youngsters around him and led us, to our great surprise, back into the theatre. Leading the way, he stepped on to the now sparsely lit stage with such certainty that the staff in charge did not dare to come over and ask us to leave. I can still remember the coffin which was lying there with the body of Titurel – I was particularly struck by his over-large head. From backstage, we descended several wooden steps down through the trapdoor underneath the stage. The lighting grew increasingly sparse, but Bruckner called out, 'Come along, gentlemen!' and led us down a further level into the cellar. So there we stood, with no idea what we were supposed to be doing. Then, suddenly, somebody shouted, 'Bruckner's disappeared!' In answer to our choruses of 'Herr Professor, Herr Professor!' we heard a faint voice calling from somewhere, 'Yes, yes, here I am!' We followed the voice and discovered the Master in a fantastic situation: he was kneeling down on the sodden clay floor, digging around in it with both hands. I was shocked, and wondered if our leader had gone mad. Some of the others obviously thought the same, as they tried to get him to stand up. He refused emphatically. We looked at each other, shaking our heads. Then finally he jumped up, covered in sweat. A thick crust of clay covered his face and hands, two great lumps of the same clinging stuff were stuck to his knees, and his sleeves and cuffs were in a similar mess. It was a bizarre spectacle. We broke out – *nolens volens* – in resounding laughter, whereupon he became very angry and – speaking through the clay, which hindered him somewhat – subjected us to a short lecture. From this we gathered that we would do better to be a little more idealistic, *nota bene* in a place which the Master himself had visited and spoken about the foundations. Furthermore, we were told that it would be wiser for us to do the same as he (i.e. Bruckner) and take some valuable souvenir home with us as well. And then we saw it: he opened his clay-covered hands and in triumphant happiness showed us – a lump of brick which he had dug from the filthy ground! He was so excited about this great idea of his and with the happy result of his excavations that we – heaven knows why – could no longer laugh. It was the ever-practical Löwe who called out. 'But, Herr Professor, what *do* you look like?' Löwe then produced a sheet of newspaper, half of which was used straight away to wrap up the precious brick, the other half had to serve as a cloth to give the Master's hands (which seemed to be encased in boxing gloves) a hurried cleaning. 'I'll take the brick back to Vienna with me.' Bruckner announced with a smile. 'It'll make a paperweight for my desk.' We ascended the steps in the same order as we had descended them: Bruckner in the lead, merrily brandishing his brick, like Parsifal with the Holy Grail. Over the excellent beer which followed, he was more talkative than I had ever seen him and was full of funny stories for the rest of the evening.

[Göllerich/Auer, 4/2, 673–6]

RICHARD AND COSIMA WAGNER

What did Wagner make of Bruckner? It is hard to find any record of his private feelings for the man. He certainly expressed admiration for the music, though, as

Robert Simpson points out in *The Essence of Bruckner*, apart from magnanimously accepting the dedication of the Third Symphony, Wagner actually did very little to help Bruckner. Cosima Wagner quotes some remarks about the symphony as a form made by Wagner in 1878, the year after the première of Bruckner's 'Wagner' Symphony, No. 3. Taken at face value, they suggest that at this time Wagner had little, if any, sympathy with the Brucknerian idea of the symphony:

Over coffee R. told me, 'I would like to write symphonies, in which I could write down ideas just as they came into my mind, as I have no lack of ideas . . . I would return to the old form of the symphony, in one movement with an andante in the middle: since Beethoven one can no longer write symphonies in four movements, they only look like imitations – as, for instance, if one were to write such big scherzos.'

[Cosima Wagner, *Die Tagebücher*, 19 November 1878, 234]

There is, however, one rather touching little entry in Cosima Wagner's diaries:

Friday 22 [April 1881]
R[ichard] dreamed that a pope who looked like the musician Bruckner came to visit him, introduced by my father (more or less the Emperor of Brazil), and when R. went to kiss his hand, His Holiness kissed him instead and took out a bottle of cognac . . .

[Cosima Wagner, *Die Tagebücher, Band* II, 729]

While Bruckner's reverence for Wagner is beyond doubt, the next reminiscence suggests that his 'thoughtlessness in his behaviour towards his best friends' (see Karl Waldeck, p. 46) could extend even to the memory of The Master himself.

FELIX WEINGARTNER

Today, Felix Weingartner (1863–1942) is remembered as one of the outstanding conductors of his age, though he longed for recognition as a composer of operas and large-scale orchestral works. He was admired above all for his conducting of the Viennese symphonic classics, especially Beethoven; his scrupulous attention to the composer's markings, especially with regard to tempo, set him in strong contrast to Hans von Bülow, whose very free interpretative style Weingartner attacked as egocentric. The encounter with Bruckner described below took place during a visit to Wagner's grave, not long after the latter's death.

As we walked towards the simple stone, someone spoke in a loud voice. Amongst the small number of people present was a small, plump man with a striking head. 'Please tell the ladies at Wahnfried', he called to the servant in attendance, 'that my —th Symphony has had great success in —' The number of the symphony and the name of the city in which it was performed have long escaped me. When the servant appeared not to understand him, he repeated his commission in more urgent tones. 'We're here to visit this grave, and we'd prefer not to have to listen to people talking about their symphonies,' I said rather loudly, and walked off, taking Reisenauer by the arm – he was as offended as I was by this lack of sensitivity. Later I came across the same small man surrounded by a flock of small boys. 'Excuse me, who is this gentleman?' I asked one of them quietly. He looked at me with some impatience. 'Don't you know Anton Bruckner?' Certainly I had heard of him, though his music was still unknown to me. Later I came to admire many of this composer's beautiful themes, but it was only with difficulty that I suppressed a feeling of aversion whenever I encountered him; the memory of his behaviour at Wagner's grave was not easily banished.

[Weingartner, *Lebenserinnerungen* (revised edition, 1928), 198–9]

Friends and Enemies

In Vienna, the Wagnerian and Brahmsian factions remained bitterly opposed almost to end of the nineteenth century. It is tempting to label the two sides respectively 'progressive' and 'conservative', though, as Sigismund Bachrich hinted earlier (p. 127), the political complexion was rather more complicated. Whatever, composers were expected to declare an allegiance, and Bruckner had placed himself firmly in the Wagnerian camp with the dedication of his Third Symphony to Wagner. This made him (wittingly or not) a member of the *avant garde*: composers like Franz Liszt and Hugo Wolf were therefore his allies, while Brahms was automatically his enemy. But how deep were these allegiances – and, indeed, how profound were the enmities? Let us take Hugo Wolf first. Carl Hruby has reported Bruckner's enthusiastic judgement of Wolf's *Lieder und Gesänge*; Anton Meissner recalls that for Bruckner, 'Wolf was the most talented of the new, young German school' [Göllenrich/Auer, 4/2, 133–6]. For his part, Wolf once wrote that 'a single cymbal clash by Bruckner is worth all four Brahms symphonies with the serenades thrown in'. Friedrich Eckstein was on friendly terms with both composers. In the next extract he analyses their relationship.

FRIEDRICH ECKSTEIN

Hugo Wolf and Anton Bruckner often met at concerts, at rehearsals and in the street. Later, Wolf was to call on Bruckner repeatedly at the Hessgasse. Whether or not all these visits were returned, I cannot tell: I can remember only one visit Bruckner in turn paid on his so-called 'Wolferl': it was while Wolf, my friends Dr Edmund Lang and his wife Marie and I were spending the summer together at Schloss 'Bellevue' near Vienna. Bruckner had come by coach to nearby Grinzing, where we collected him and took him up the steep path through the vineyards to Bellevue. There we spent a wonderful summer evening drinking glasses of Grinzinger wine in the open air beneath the old linden trees, with the lights of Vienna flickering in the distance. After supper, Bruckner sat down at the piano and played passages from his Eighth Symphony with complete abandon. Then, in deepest darkness, we brought him back to down to Grinzing, surrounded by swarms of buzzing fireflies, and toasted his impending journey together at the 'Heuriger'. Bruckner returned by coach to the city, while an elated Hugo Wolf headed back with us to our country retreat.

And yet despite their many cordial meetings, Bruckner and Wolf never really became close friends, not because of the obvious age difference, but rather since there were so few spiritual points of contact between them. Wolf had little sympathy for Bruckner's strict Catholic devotion; he was a man of the world through and through, a sound, sensitive connoisseur of German and much foreign literature: he had a wide variety of philosophical interests: he knew the writings of Schopenhauer thoroughly, and he had been seized by an unbridled passion for Nietzsche's *Zarathustra* and *The Case of Wagner* almost as soon as they had appeared in print. I still remember a heated discussion between Wolf, Josef Schalk and myself about Nietzsche and Wagner and their relation to the world-views of Hegel and Feuerbach. Bruckner showed not the slightest interest in any of this. His was not a literary mind, and whereas Hugo Wolf would bury himself in Jean Paul, devour the poems of Leopardi or the Spanish mystics or similarly busy himself with the English humorists, the German romantics or Greek tragedies, it was all lost on Bruckner. His disposition was simple, thoroughly childlike: he was completely absorbed in the magical, labyrinthine world of his contrapuntal architecture, which now glowed like the setting sun filtered through stained glass, and now sent gloomy shadows falling on dark vaults and fearsome crypts.

The deeper he lost himself in this internal warp and weft of interweaving musical voices, the more oblivious he became to anything that might draw him away from this world.

Consequently Hugo Wolf distanced himself, purely in musical respects, from Bruckner for a while; and when the revised version of the First Symphony (C minor) was given its first performance, he made some highly sceptical comments about this work in one of his letters. But none of this prevented Wolf from recognizing with growing clarity that Anton Bruckner was one of the greatest musicians of all time; and when he heard several years later that the Master's health was rapidly deteriorating, he felt the urgent need to see him once more. At the time, Wolf was living with our friends Professor Karl Mayerder and his wife Rosa in the Plössgasse, quite close to the Belvedere Park, where free accommodation had been furnished for Bruckner in a small annexe of the Palace. He came back from this brief visit deeply shaken, and described it to Rosa Mayerder, still highly moved what he had just experienced.

When Wolf entered the apartment at the Belvedere, Bruckner's housekeeper informed him that it was no longer possible to speak to the Master as his mind was failing. But Wolf, undeterred, crept on tiptoe to the half-open sick-room door and stole a glance inside. What he saw he found deeply and uniquely moving: in a simple iron bed, almost buried in pillows, lay Anton Bruckner, his countenance pale and shrunken, his eyes fixed on the ceiling, with a blissful smile on his lips, which moved almost imperceptibly as though mouthing some seraphic song; and all the time his wasted right hand beat time softly on the counterpane, the forefinger outstretched, as if in response to a music that he alone was able to hear, transported beyond all earthly things, and already halfway to eternity.

[Eckstein, 180–2]

But there might have been another, more personal, reason why Bruckner ignored Wolf's discussions with Schalk.

MAX VON OBERLEITHNER

When I bought him news of the Wagner Society, he complained that Josef Schalk neglected him in favour of Hugo Wolf. Bruckner was full of unjustified jealousy, and he could not understand how anyone could place Wolf on the same level as Schubert, let alone above him.

[Oberleithner, 33]

Reports of relations between Bruckner and Liszt are similarly contradictory, though it seems that their first meeting was cordial enough, and that up to this point Bruckner would have counted himself one of Liszt's admirers.

ENGELBERT LANZ

Engelbert Lanz (1820–1904) was a music-teacher and composer from Linz. He helped prepare the first performance of Bruckner's E minor Mass in 1869, and seven years earlier conducted the première of Bruckner's Festive Cantata *Preiset den Herrn* ('Praise the Lord'), for four-part male chorus, woodwind, brass and timpani. Bruckner's Linz friend Ignaz Dorn had introduced him to the music of Liszt; it was Lanz who provided the introduction to the man himself.

I was with Bruckner during the holidays; it was then that he expressed the wish to meet Liszt, who was then staying in Vienna. 'If only I knew how to go about it,' he said. 'That's not as difficult as it sounds,' I replied. 'If it's all right with you I'll arrange it.' 'How? – can you do that?' 'Yes I can, and with luck the opportunity will arise soon. I'll write to my cousin in Vienna at once. He's a good friend and admirer of Liszt. I'll ask him to organize it.'

Bruckner looked forward enthusiastically to the realization of this plan. I sent the letter the next day, and immediately it brought the reply for which we had hoped. Bruckner insisted that I accompany him, and so we arrived in Vienna at the time fixed by my dear cousin, who was waiting for us at the station. Having told us all we needed to know, including the information that Herr Liszt was looking forward to meeting us, Bruckner and I arrived at the hotel where the famous man was staying, the 'Schottenhof'.

Bruckner was visibly excited, I no less. The servant announced our arrival. A few minutes later we stood facing the tall, lean figure of Franz Liszt. Bruckner, as shy as ever, remained practically in the doorway. We bowed deeply. The Master stepped towards us in a friendly manner.

'Herr von Liszt,' I began, 'may I have the honour of introducing myself, my name is Lanz.' – 'Ah, Herr Lanz,' Liszt replied, stretching out both his hands towards me. 'And here', I continued, indicating my friend, 'is Herr Bruckner.' 'Bruckner?' – Liszt smiled; you could tell from his expression that he was pleasantly surprised – 'Ah, Herr Bruckner!' he replied, greeting him in the same kind way and shaking his hand vigorously. 'I've already heard a lot about you,' continued Liszt in his own particular dialect; 'I am truly delighted to meet you!'

With these words, he very politely invited us to take a seat, after which a lively conversation unfolded between the two Masters, which lasted for some time.

[Göllerich/Auer, 4/1, 204–6]

The reference to Liszt in Friedrich Eckstein's story about the Adagio of the Eighth Symphony (p. 105) suggests that Bruckner became aware of profound differences between his art and that of his contemporary and fellow Wagnerian. That suggestion is reinforced by Eckstein's next recollection.

FRIEDRICH ECKSTEIN

On my arrival one day at the Hessgasse, Bruckner handed me a very full letter from Hans von Wolzogen in Bayreuth, in which Richard Wagner's famous friend and adviser enquired whether Bruckner might be interested in composing an oratorio on St Francis's 'Canticle of the Sun'. A copy of the Italian poem was included with the letter. Since Bruckner had no grasp of Italian, I read him the opening lines to give him some idea of the sound of the verse. The hymn begins with these words:

Altissimo omnipotente bon signore:
Tue son laude la gloria et l'honore et ogni benedictione.

Since Bruckner also wanted to see the best available translation of the poem, I brought him the much-admired version by Johann Heinrich Schlosser, the famous translator of devotional songs:

Höchster, allmächtiger gütiger Herr:
Dein ist der Preis, die Herrlichkeit und die Ehre und jegliche Benedeiung.

[Exalted, almighty, gracious Lord,
Thine is the praise, the glory and the honour and every blessing]

This is how the first two lines sound in Schlosser's somewhat wooden translation. Bruckner was astonished when I informed him that Franz Liszt had already set the 'Canticle of the Sun' in a version for baritone solo, men's chorus, organ and orchestra, and he asked me if I would lend him the score. But when I called on him again several days later he declared adamantly that he could not possibly work on the hymn; it meant nothing to him, and so he could not set it to music. That Liszt had found it accessible came as no surprise; but his own way of making music was quite different.

Since then I have often wondered whether Bruckner's rejection of the 'Canticle of the Sun' might not be linked with his upbringing in Upper Austria and the time he spent under the influence of the Augustinians – that perhaps he found the whole Franciscan tradition somewhat alien, while for someone like Liszt it would have been utterly captivating.

[Eckstein, 140–42]

Some more explicitly negative remarks about Liszt are quoted in Göllerich/Auer. Apparently Bruckner told his pupil Franz Marschner that 'Liszt is more of a Master of homophonic style, not of counterpoint.' We also learn that Bruckner 'thought little of Liszt's thematic working – the fugues in St Elizabeth and Christus did not impress him, though he was delighted with some individual sections. He loved the two great masses, though not the Credo of the Coronation Mass.' A little later comes the revelation that Bruckner placed Berlioz 'far higher than Liszt', and that he was 'particularly impressed by Berlioz's counterpoint and instumentation – especially in the *Requiem*' (Göllerich/Auer, 4/2, 169).

But Bruckner was evidently capable of lowering his critical defences, as the next story reveals.

AUGUST STRADAL

During a performance of Liszt's 'Tasso', I had the good fortune to sit next to Bruckner. It was clear that Bruckner was deeply moved by the work, but he suddenly asked me what the word 'Tasso' meant. I explained to him the suffering and hostilities which the immortal poet of Ferrara had been forced to tolerate; I described to him Tasso's death and how his body was crowned on the Capitol. As I finished my explanation, I noticed tears in Bruckner's eyes. He cried out, 'That's me!' I told him that in his work 'Tasso, Lamento e trionfo' Liszt had not intended to describe in music the individual case of Tasso, but that through this composition he had wanted to set to music the archetypal fate of every creative genius who invents something new.

[Göllerich/Auer, 4/2, 167–8]

And what of Liszt's attitude to Bruckner? Stradal recalls a meeting between the two composers in 1885.

In Vienna, Liszt paid a visit to the Schottenkirche, where Anton Bruckner usually went to worship. One morning, Dr Standhartner, the long-standing friend of Richard Wagner, Schoeniach, the well-known writer on music, and I were together with Liszt when Anton Bruckner appeared, in an old-fashioned tailcoat, a collapsible opera hat in his hand. Bruckner's dress was not altogether in keeping with the times, for with the tailcoat he wore a pair of short, grey breeches, from which protruded a enormous pair of drainpipe boots (the kind manufactured at St Florian). We all smiled, especially when Bruckner humbly addressed Liszt with the words, 'Your Grace, Herr Canon'. Bruckner had come to Liszt to ask him to recommend a performance of the Seventh Symphony (with Mottl conducting) at the Karlsruhe Composers' Assembly (*Tonkunstlerversammlung*). Liszt seemed to find it hard to refuse Bruckner's request, but it wasn't possible to perform the entire work, since the programme for the Composers' Assembly had already been decided. Liszt, who was normally open to any petition, seemed somewhat put out by Bruckner's repeated requests. From this short meeting between the two Masters, I sensed that Liszt had no great sympathy for Bruckner as an artist; though when Bruckner left, Liszt was very friendly with him and promised to grant his request, if it were still possible. However, at the Composers' Assembly only the Adagio of the Seventh was played. On the return journey from Karlsruhe, Liszt did comment favourably on the Adagio, yet there was still a feeling that the work had not particularly impressed him. Apart from the Adagio of the Seventh, Liszt heard two movements of the *Romantic* Symphony and the whole of the Quintet at the Sonderhausen Composers' Assembly in 1886 (less than two months before his death). At the performance of the *Romantic* Symphony I sat in the second row, behind Liszt, who was next to his biographer Lina Ramann. When the second movement was over, Ramann remarked to Liszt. 'This is like orchestrated Clementi.'* Liszt responded with his nasal 'Pah, Pah', but said nothing to contradict Ramann's opinion. The Quintet, despite its wonderful Adagio, also made no impression. By this time, Liszt was already very ill and therefore less capable of grasping anything new and strange. To my knowledge, he heard nothing of Bruckner's apart from the Adagio of the Seventh, the two movements of the *Romantic* Symphony and the Quintet. Bruckner did in fact dedicate his Second Symphony to Liszt, but later withdrew the dedication. Liszt never knew the symphony. For Liszt, it was inconceivable that anyone could write symphonies after Beethoven's Ninth, since this, for him, was the culmination of the form. It was only through the medium of the symphonic poem, programme music, that he believed the way to new artistic creations could be found.

[August Stradal, *Erinnerungen an Franz Liszt*, 89–91]

Now here is another another version of the Second Symphony dedication story.

*Apparently Liszt considered Clementi 'a mere craftsman' – see Adrian Williams, *Portrait of Liszt*, Oxford, 1990, 634.

AUGUST GÖLLERICH/MAX AUER

At the end of April, Franz Liszt made his usual Easter trip to the 'Schottenhof'. Bruckner went to visit him, taking with him the score of his Second Symphony – one of his favourite 'children' – and asked Liszt if he could dedicate it to him, 'because it needs a good father'. Liszt was happy to agree, and intended to take the work back to Weimar with him, where he could look through it properly. Liszt, in the haste of travel and the confusion of constant overwork, then forgot this intention, as Bruckner discovered by chance a year later. Deeply hurt, he immediately withdrew the kind dedication.

When Göllerich attempted to arouse Liszt's interest in Bruckner, the usually mild man cut him short with the words, 'If your friend approaches me with the dedication "Your Grace's humble church musician", that's quite enough for me!' On this occasion the overly refined cosmopolitan was unable to overcome his personal dislike of the unaffected, natural and childlike Bruckner.

[Göllerich/Auer, 4/2, 166–7]

Bruckner's offical arch-rival in Vienna was Johannes Brahms. Naturally, there was bound to be an element of competition between two eminent symphonists working in the same city, and in public at least the war of words could be bitter. But there was a noticeable cooling off in both composers' last years: in 1891 Brahms went so far as to recommend Bruckner for a commission from the Vienna Singverein (the result was *Psalm 150*), and in 1893 he was seen warmly applauding a performance of Bruckner's F minor Mass. Two years later, Bruckner was created an honorary member of the Gesellschaft der Musikfreunde. Brahms was asked to add his signature to an official address to Bruckner by the Vienna Composer's Society (*Tonkunstlerverein*). Richard Heuberger records his response.

RICHARD HEUBERGER

Brahms told me that he would not sign the address to Bruckner because it he found it badly drawn up and shabbily produced. 'Something like this should be decent and serious!' Jenner, the secretary of the Society, seemed quite proud of his slapdash job. 'Are you here to play the fool?' he asked, and made all sorts of corrections to the text, bringing in something about the students, Bruckner's popularity, and so on. 'I certainly wouldn't go through thick and thin for Bruckner, but the fellow is damnably serious about what he does, and he deserves to be honoured for it.'

[Richard Heuberger, *Erinnerungen an Johannes Brahms*, 71–2]

But the cease-fire was a long time coming. Max von Oberleithner describes the Bruckner–Brahms relationship in earlier years.

MAX VON OBERLEITHNER

Like almost every composer, Brahms was possessed by jealousy and someone else's success always displeased him, even though he had nothing to fear from it. I myself often saw how he sat during a Bruckner performance in the director's box at the Gesellschaft der Musikfreunde, bent right forward, watching the orchestra, his face turning red . . .

Bruckner had more reason to be jealous, given his rival's high standing throughout the musical world; but he never uttered a malicious word against his enemy. The following story, related to me by Herr Almeroth, shows how resigned Bruckner was. Once, when Bruckner was with friends at the swimming-bath in Steyr, the conversation came round to Brahms. Bruckner sighed deeply – 'Yes indeed, Brahms!' and dived into the water, remaining hidden from sight for some time. This was how he suppressed his hostile feelings; Brahms's behaviour, on the other hand, was not at all in accordance with his eminent position.

In life they both had much in common. Brahms too lived as a bachelor, and as regards clothing he also liked wide trousers, a comfortable overcoat and boots. To be sure, he usually carried an umbrella, while Bruckner relied on the enormous brim of his soft hat to protect him from the rain.

Both of them loved to take a fresh glass of draught Pilsner beer in a good restaurant, though not necessarily in the better rooms, rather somewhere near the place where the beer came direct from the cellar; in the 'Red Hedgehog', this would have been the ground floor. There, so the story goes, the two Masters once met, both accompanied by a few supporters. Probably Bruckner was already sitting at the table when Brahms entered, and, as there was no other place free in that small room, he sat down with him. Bruckner, I suspect, would have preferred to go to another restaurant. At first the atmosphere was chilly and unpleasant; it wasn't until both composers ordered smoked meat with cabbage and dumplings that the ice finally broke. Bruckner himself told me that it was during this encounter that Brahms had remarked, in his usual coarse way, 'I didn't think much of your Third Symphony', to which Bruckner had replied, 'The Master Richard Wagner thought a lot of it.' This meeting must have taken place long before my time, because later on Bruckner could never have eaten anything as heavy as smoked meat for dinner.

[Oberleithner, 44–6]

One of the problems with the 'Red Hedgehog' story is that there are so many versions of it, almost all of them second-hand reports, and each one subtly different. (Carl Hruby states bluntly that the alleged 'meeting' in the Red Hedgehog never took place.) But the next account does appear to be based on personal experience.

AUGUST STRADAL

Brahms treated Bruckner with great condescension, and a coldness towards him penetrated right through to his heart, whereas Bruckner, in his childlike simplicity, often revealed his innermost thoughts. Once, he was even so careless as to complain to Brahms about Hanslick! Bruckner's deference towards the reserved Brahms always irritated me; once he actually fetched his beer for him from the bar as though he were a waiter. Only on one occasion did the conversation between them become worrying. It was after a performance of Bruckner's Eighth Symphony, when Bruckner and Brahms met in the restaurant the 'Red Hedgehog'. Without thinking, Bruckner asked Brahms if he had liked the Eighth, to which Brahms answered, 'My dear Bruckner, I don't understand your symphonies!' Bruckner replied, 'I've exactly the same problem with yours.'

[Göllerich/Auer, 4/2, 690]

FRANZ MARSCHNER

The pianist, organist and composer Franz Marschner (1855–1932) attended Bruckner's lectures in counterpoint at the Vienna Conservatory, and later became a friend of the composer. He records two occasions when Bruckner did not suppress his feelings about Brahms.

During one of the Hellmesberger Quartet's evening recitals, a piece by Anton Dvořák was played – probably for the first time in Vienna. When we left, Bruckner spoke extremely disparagingly, indeed scornfully, about this quartet, as he mistakenly called it.

He was obviously annoyed by the financial support given to Dvořák, while he himself was ignored. He was not very pleasant about Brahms either. When we heard Brahms's First Violin Sonata in the Great Hall of the Musikverein, he claimed that it just followed in the wake of Mendelssohn. During a performance of Mozart's String Quintet in G minor, in the E flat major slow movement to be precise, he said to me excitedly, 'Has Brahms ever thought of such a melody?' He was very bitter about Brahms's behaviour towards the young Hans Rott. Hynais and I accompanied Bruckner to the funeral of this young composer, of whom Bruckner was especially fond. It seemed that he attributed the young man's illness and death to the harshness of Brahms's judgement on one of Rott's compositions. I shall never forget the marked contrast between the peaceful aura of the dead man in the open coffin and the impassioned behaviour of the Master. On the way home his feelings broke out in these words, 'Brahms is an extraordinary musician and a great contrapuntist, but . . .' and he continued in great emotion, 'I'm going to tell him – sir, you're not a composer, you're just a craftsman!' The following thoughts, which Bruckner expressed on that same occasion, suggest that this is not to be taken too literally – 'Anyone who wants to listen to music in order to relax will enjoy the music of Brahms; but anyone who wants to be gripped by music cannot be satisfied by his works.' In speaking of music which 'gripped', he was obviously thinking of the new school, and especially of his own.

[Göllerich/Auer, 4/2, 130–32]

ANTON MEISSNER

The son of a Viennese master-butcher, Anton Meissner (1855–1932) studied first at commercial college; then, in 1876, he became a pupil of Bruckner at the Conservatory (Franz Schalk was one of his classmates), though the lectures he refers to here took place at the University. Meissner remained close to Bruckner, and during the composer's final illness he worked as his private secretary. He recalls one of Bruckner's more aphoristic judgements on Brahms, as well as his opinions on several other composers.

When the lecture had finished I would go and see Bruckner, whose greeting was usually so exuberant that my cheeks were often red from the kisses he gave me with his smoothly shaven face. Having greeted me, he would take out the piece of notepaper which accompanied him everywhere, walk over to the wretched, out-of-tune piano and play me excerpts from the *Te Deum* and the Seventh Symphony, which he was working on at the time. He would then ask me which particular version he should choose. He tried out this experiment with many people, even with Frau Kathi. In this, he reminded me strongly of Molière, who also read his works to his cook for her to assess. I once played for him Liszt's Paganini-Etude in E flat major, the fugato of which interested him, as well as the Scherzo from his own Third Symphony (D minor), which he felt conductors always performed too quickly. I also played

Chopin's study in C minor for him, a piece which he greatly admired and valued. For that, I rose greatly in his esteem and received a flood of kisses. By now the University porter had usually appeared in the doorway several times, which meant that it was time to go. Bruckner did not like having to leave this familiar and much-loved place, where he had often had magnificent flashes of inspiration and where, tucked away upstairs, he could work more quietly than anywhere. We would then wander through the town, or in spring though the Stadtpark, where he liked to stay a while by the lake and watch the storks and the swans, happily remembering that he too had been a good swimmer. Whilst we were walking he would often tell me about his compositions, saying for example that he was composing the *Te Deum* purely for God, or that whilst he was composing the Seventh Symphony he had had a premonition of the death of King Ludwig II of Bavaria, whose artistic talents and splendid patronage of the arts he greatly admired. I remember that during one such walk I asked him what he thought of the work of Brahms. He pondered deeply over this question for a while and then said: 'You know, Anton, we two are fiery individuals, and Catholics. Brahms is for cold-natured people and Protestants!' At this time the Ring tetralogy was being performed (then still a rare event), and we sometimes saw each other there in the fourth gallery. The 'Woodbird', the Rhinemaidens' trio and 'Siegfried's Death' particularly appealed to him. He also boasted that, while he was living in Linz, he had attended the first performance of *Tristan* in Munich. When it came to judging other composers he was restrained, careful and sometimes sarcastic.

In addition to Beethoven, who as we know was called a 'musical swine' after the first performance of *Fidelio* – a remark which almost always moved Bruckner to tears – as well as Bach, Haydn, Mozart and Schubert (whose songs Bruckner studied in detail), the Master was completely wrapped up in Wagner. He did once say to me that Chopin was 'extremely interesting'. Unfortunately he usually used this stereotypical and often sarcastic expression to describe the work of Liszt. As far as I know, he liked only the Gretchen movement from the *Faust* Symphony. In 1895 he also dismissed Richard Strauss's *Till Eulenspiegel* as 'extremely interesting'. But he admitted to me, after the first performance of the work by the Philharmonic (the *Romantic* Symphony was also on the programme), that he had snoozed a little.

[Göllerich/Auer, 4/2, 133–6]

FRANZ MARSCHNER

Franz Marschner continues with more of Bruckner's idiosyncratic judgements on his contemporaries – performers as well as composers.

Apart from Richard Wagner, whom he described as the greatest of all Masters at a meeting of the Wagner Society, he told me that no other contemporary composer had impressed him. Included in this damning judgement was Liszt, whom Bruckner had just visited while the latter was staying in Vienna. I think that on that occasion Liszt had accepted the dedication of one of Bruckner's early symphonies.

During a cycle of Rubinstein's works he delivered this unmistakable side-swipe, 'Since Wagner's death the greatest artist is Anton Rubinstein.' He was of course referring only to Rubinstein the pianist, because Rubinstein the composer was far too conservative for his liking. This is illustrated by Bruckner's judgement on Rubinstein's *Nero*, which was performed at that time – 'What can you do when the new direction is being completely avoided?' This attribution of greatness to Rubinstein is interesting because – as with Liszt's views – it appears to derive from an equal valuation of the productive and reproductive arts. When I asked his opinion of Bülow as a conductor he replied, 'Bülow is the number one conductor in the world.' It seemed to me that this comment was made partly with Hans Richter in mind – Bruckner was not particularly pleased with Richter's performances of his works. He also complained a good deal about the members of the Philharmonic. He felt that he had not only been neglected but also misunderstood and treated with disrespect. He once claimed that Richter did not understand the contrapuntal aspect of his symphonies. According to Bruckner, the only thing he had learned from Richter was about certain instrumental doublings, which he had introduced when Richter criticized his music for lacking effect. The strong self-esteem he understandably possessed often helped to counter feelings of dejection and extreme doubt – the feeling that perhaps his opponents were right after all. He would comfort himself by saying, 'Even if I can't compare myself to Schubert and the other great Masters, I still know I'm "somebody" and that what I do matters.'

[Göllerich/Auer, 4/2, 132–3]

It is difficult to say how much Schubert Bruckner knew. Many of the larger-scale choral, orchestral and chamber works were not published until quite late in Bruckner's life. At about nineteen, he became acquainted with Karoline Eberstaller of Steyr, who had been one of Schubert's duet partners; she introduced Bruckner to some of Schubert's four-hand piano music. Bruckner's Viennese champion Johann Herbeck conducted the first performance of Schubert's 'Unfinished' Symphony in 1865; even if Bruckner did not hear that, or any subsequent performance, it is by no means improbable that Herbeck showed him the score.

Bruckner certainly knew the symphonies of Beethoven. Hearing the Ninth in 1866 was a seminal musical experience. But according to Karl Waldeck, it was the *Eroica* (No. 3) that Bruckner rated highest. Bruckner's own copy of the score shows how intensively he analysed the harmonic and periodic structure of this symphony. The *Eroica* figures prominently in the next reminiscence.

CARL HRUBY

In his younger days, Bruckner's robust sense of humour and natural cheerfulness had enabled him to endure many insults and injuries, but as the years passed he became increasingly embittered and morose. At first he had not taken much notice of critical attacks, but as he grew older the continual hostility of the press made him more and more sensitive. By the second year of our acquaintance, he had already changed markedly. He would often sit for whole minutes, a hand resting on the piano, his head lowered, staring at the floor and saying not a word. Then he would launch passionately into a sentence that seemed to have been plucked from the middle of a conversation and stressed only to bring out its meaning. (Perhaps he had continued the conversation for a while in his head.) Here is one example. We entered the classroom; Bruckner was sitting at the piano, lost in thought, and barely responded to our greeting. Suddenly he blurted out these curious words: 'Those people . . .' (by which he meant a certain species of critic) ' . . . say that my ideas aren't consistent. My God! Even in Wagner the ideas aren't all equally splendid.' And then his conversation turned to Beethoven.

Beethoven! Beethoven! For Bruckner he was the incarnation of everything lofty and sublime in music. He connected that hallowed name with all the twists of fortune in his own life, and at crucial moments he often asked how Beethoven would have behaved in the same situation. When, after a performance of one of Bruckner's symphonies, the rabble again attacked him as one man – at their head, of course, the Fichtegasse's champion of 'Beauty in Music'* – we tried to comfort him by invoking posterity: that time in the future when everything beautiful and truly great would be recognized and judged calmly and objectively. Bruckner listened quietly for a while and then said in a deeply downcast voice: 'Yes, but by then it will be "too late!", as the great Beethoven said when they brought him wine on his deathbed.' Then he shared with us the following – to my knowledge, unknown – reminiscence of Beethoven that he had heard from Rotter (an old Viennese musician, recently deceased), who in turn had got it from the famous violinist Schuppanzigh, with whom Rotter had spent a good deal of time in his youth.

Schuppanzigh had once called on Beethoven to go walking with him in the countryside around Vienna. As he entered the room, he saw Beethoven leaning with his back against the window, holding a newspaper in his hand. With tear-filled eyes, he handed it to Schuppanzigh with the words: 'Humanity – so stupid, oh, so

*Hanslick.

stupid!' (apparently Beethoven spoke bad German).* It was the paper in which some erstwhile Hanslick had, after the first performance of the *Eroica* Symphony, called Beethoven a 'musical swine'! The tremendous dissonances of the development, which herald the collapse of ancient injustice and the glorious ascent of the young Napoleon, offended the fine sensibilities of this ass-eared critic. If you had not seen and heard it for yourself, you could hardly imagine the power of expression Bruckner brought to this little story!

The day Beethoven's remains were exhumed, Bruckner invited me to go with him to the old Währinger cemetery. Those who took part in the ceremony will no doubt remember the unforgettable moment when, just as the coffin was being lifted up and solemn silence had descended all around, a nightingale suddenly launched into a torrent of sobbing notes from a nearby tree – as if in a final tribute to the great mastersinger. The powerful effect was soon spoiled when the representatives of the City of Vienna began squabbling about whether the coffin should be opened in the cemetery or later, in the chapel. In the end, they decided on the first option. – Bruckner stood in front of me and stared into the coffin, deeply moved.

On the way home, his mood was very serious. The gloomy solemnity of the occasion appeared to have shaken him to the core. He hardly spoke ten words. Suddenly he noticed that one of the lenses had fallen out of his pince-nez. 'I think', he said, brimming over with joy, 'it must've fallen into Beethoven's coffin while I was leaning over.' It delighted him to know that his eyeglass was buried with Beethoven.

After a performance of the *Eroica* by the Philharmonic which Bruckner had heard, as usual, standing behind the orchestral

*'Humanity . . .' The German original is '*Die Menschheit – so dumm, ach, so dumm*!' – conversational, but hardly 'bad German'.

N.B. Hruby adds this note about the later conversation in Gause's Restaurant: 'I wrote down the whole of this conversation that same evening, as soon as I got home. The reader will perhaps notice a difference in the reported speech; this was a peculiarity of Bruckner. Most of the time he spoke in a kind of half-dialect; sometimes High German, but whenever he got excited, then it was pure Upper Austrian.' Representing this 'half-dialect' convincingly in English proved beyond the powers of this translator.

platform, I went with him to Gause's Restaurant. After any performance of a Beethoven symphony he was always tremendously excited, but I had never seen him like this before, nor have I since. Every nerve trembled. After he had spent a while sunk in thought, his gaze as it were turned inwards, he suddenly broke the silence: 'I think, if Beethoven were still alive today, and I went to him, showed him my Seventh Symphony and said to him, "Don't you think, Herr von Beethoven, that the Seventh isn't as bad as certain people make it out to be – those people who make an example of it and portray me as an idiot – " then, maybe, Beethoven might take me by the hand and say, "My dear Bruckner, don't bother yourself about it. It was no better for me, and the same gentlemen who use me as a stick to beat you with still don't really understand my last quartets, however much they may pretend to." Then I might go on and say, "Please excuse me, Herr von Beethoven, if I've gone beyond you . . ." (Bruckner was referring to his use of form!) " . . . but I've always said that a true artist can work out his own form and then stick to it." ' In the Gasthaus, over a glass of the 'precious Pilsner', he opened out completely, and in the course of the conversation he came round to Hanslick and his consorts. 'That Hanslick's always saying that I've no form – no form! I mean, if someone could sound out the Herr Doctor to find out what he means by form, well – I think – he wouldn't be so sure himself. Doesn't an artist have the right to chose the form for his works that suits him? But with Hanslick it's another story: he's so full of spite. I came very near to being one of his "beloved children" once, but then I went and committed an unforgivable sin by dedicating my Third Symphony to the Master . . .' (Bruckner never called Wagner anything other than 'the Master') ' . . . and then came what really annoyed him: against his will, they made me a teacher at the University. He'll never forgive me that – he told me that himself. What he's really looking for is someone he can use as a trump card against the hated Wagner, and that's why he's made such a fuss of Brahms – it's because he couldn't use me.' With a delightful wink in my direction, he continued, 'What I mean is that Hanslick understands Brahms about as much as he understands Wagner, me or anyone else. And when it comes to counterpoint – well, the Herr Doctor knows as much about counterpoint as a chimney-sweep knows about astronomy!' And little by little he talked himself round into a more humorous mood – he was the old Bruckner again.

[Hruby, 19–23]

ALEXANDER FRÄNKEL

Dr Alexander Fränkel's experience was obviously rather different from that of Anton Meissner and Franz Marschner. But he does recall a rare comment by Bruckner on another of his contemporaries.

I am in no position whatsoever to comment on Bruckner as a musician. I was however greatly displeased by his marked indifference towards the musical productions of his time. He appeared to feel absolutely no need to become acquainted with the works of other Masters, and I genuinely believe that of all contemporary composers he really knew only Richard Wagner. I remember the following episode: it was a beautiful evening in summer and we were strolling through the Prater, Bruckner walking in his customary manner, his hat in his hand and his arm under that of his companion. In the distance we heard military music coming from a garden of one of the inns. We drew closer and closer to it until we could hear quite clearly what was being played. Bruckner stood still, listening attentively, until the piece was over. 'Herr Doctor,' he said after a while, as if still pondering deeply over what he had just heard, 'that was lovely, what was it?' It was the Miserere from Verdi's *Trovatore*.

[Göllerich/Auer, 4/2, 29]

Wagner might have been Bruckner's idol amongst his contempories, but even 'the Master of the Nibelungen' could not eclipse the gods of the musical past. Karl Waldeck writes, 'When I asked Bruckner once which three works he rated most highly he told me: Mozart's *Requiem*, the *Eroica* Symphony and the Funeral March from *Götterdämmerung*.' [Gräflinger, 116] (Fascinatingly, death is either the dominant theme or a strong presence in all three.) Bruckner's reverence for Mozart has been mentioned by Franz Marschner, and Carl Hruby has had plenty to tell us about Bruckner's attitude to Beethoven. Max von Oberleithner listed 'hearing Schubert *Lieder*' amongst the young Bruckner's formative influences (p. 9); Anton Meissner told us that Bruckner studied Schubert's songs 'in detail' (p. 155). A Schubert song turns up in the next reminiscence. Friedrich Eckstein is describing a journey by sleigh to Heiligenkreuz and Klosterneuberg.

FRIEDRICH ECKSTEIN

That winter excursion remains one of my most treasured memories. I will never forget the moment when we slid past the last houses of Heiligenstadt, through deep snow and piercing cold, the blizzard whirling about us, pressed close together and wrapped heavily in furs.

Suddenly a crow flew low across our path, wings outstretched, whereupon Bruckner bent towards me and sang, in a soft, sorrowful voice, the opening line of that immortal Schubert song: 'Eine Krähe war mit mir aus der Stadt gezogen'* – 'A crow went with me as I left the city.'

[Eckstein, *Erinnerungen an Anton Bruckner*, 21–2]

KARL KOBALD

The music-teacher and writer Karl Kobald (1876–1957) studied music privately with Guido Alder and then at the Vienna Conservatory, though not with Bruckner. He was Music Adviser to the Austrian Ministry of Education from 1918, and was President of the Akademie für Musik und darstellende Kunst ('Academy of Music and the Performing Arts') in 1932–38 and 1945–47 – i.e. before and after the Nazi occupation. In 1924 he brought out a collection of articles on Bruckner. *In Memorian Anton Bruckner*, in which he included his own reminiscences in an essay entitled 'Bruckneriana'. Kobald first encountered Bruckner in the late 1880s, when he was member of the Vienna Boys Choir.

*'Die Krähe', No. 15 from the song cycle *Winterreise*.

In those days, the Master often came to our school. At the time we were learning his great Mass [in E minor]. He listened to our rehearsals and gave us instructions for the performance. Once he appeared carrying a huge rucksack from which he removed a tremendous cake. Beaming all over his face, he cut it himself and divided between us boys – it was a thanks-offering for learning his work so diligently. On another occasion, Bruckner, that great friend of children, took several of us with him for a Sunday afternoon stroll. If I remember rightly, it was after a performance of the great E flat major Mass by Schubert. Bruckner led us to Lichtenthal, to the church where Schubert had sung as a boy and played the organ, and from there to Schubert's birthplace at the Himmelpfortgrund. It was beautiful day in May, and as we stood in the picturesque old courtyard of the Schubert-house, Bruckner told us about 'Franzl' Schubert. We formed a circle around the Master, and to his delight we sang the old Schubert song 'Am Brunnen vor dem Tore'* in our bright, clear, boys' voices.

[Kobald, 135–6]

JOSEF HOFFMAN

Josef Hoffman was choirmaster at the Evangelical Church in Linz, and director of the Church School. He remembers an occasion when Bruckner went out of his way to hear Hoffman's congregation sing a famous chorale by J. S. Bach. The keyboard works of Bach had been an important part of Bruckner's musical education since his studies with August Dürrnberger at the age of sixteen, but opportunities to hear the sacred music would have been relatively rare; and as a strict nineteenth-century Catholic, Bruckner would have felt uncomfortable about even entering a Protestant church.

Bruckner took a keen interest in the chorale *O Haupt voll Blut und Wunden* – 'O sacred head sore wounded' – so well loved amongst Evangelical congregations. Once, while I was with him at the organ during a service (in the old cathedral), he made me

*'Der Lindenbaum', No. 5 from *Winterreise*; evidently this was an arrangement.

sing the opening line of this hymn – very quietly – at the conclusion, even though he knew it very well, whereupon he made these seven notes the subject of a magnificent free fugue.

He wanted to hear this chorale sung by the congregation, so he asked me to tell him, as soon as I knew, the next time it would be heard at the Evangelical Church in Linz (unfortunately I can no longer remember the year). I was soon able to oblige him, and on the day itself (it was during Lent) he arrived, just as I was finishing the prelude to the service. He came in through the choir doors, bent low – probably to attract as little attention as possible – sat down near the organ and listened devoutly to the singing in the church. I invited him to accompany the hymn at the organ, but he gracefully declined. After hearing four verses, he expressed his satisfaction with the words, 'Ah, that's beautiful', and left the church as modestly and inconspicuously as he had entered it.

[Gräflinger, 96]

IV

A CONTRACT WITH GOD

One work dominated Bruckner's last decade: the Ninth Symphony – the work he intended to dedicate '*dem lieben Gott*' ('to the dear Lord'). It was evidently intended to be his *magnum opus*, conceived on an even grander scale than the monumental Eighth Symphony: a 'Ninth' inviting comparison with that of Beethoven. Bruckner began it in 1887; the finale was still incomplete in full score when he died, nine years later. Revisions of the Eighth, First and Third symphonies held up composition in the early stages; later, declining physical and mental health made work increasingly arduous. Characteristically, Bruckner seems to have talked about this great project, and played extracts from it, whenever he had the strength and a willing audience. One account has already been given by Max von Oberleither (pp. 94–6); we continue with two more.

JEAN LOUIS NICODÉ

Conductor, composer and professor of piano at Dresden Conservatory, Jean Louis Nicodé (1853–1919), directed the Dresden Philharmonic concerts from 1885 to 1888. An enthusiastic advocate of Wagner and Bruckner, he conducted the Dresden premières of Bruckner's Eighth (27 August 1895) and Seventh (15 March 1887) Symphonies. It is the latter performance Nicodé refers to in the text below. The visit to Bruckner he describes took place in March 1891, when Nicodé was staying in Vienna for a performance of his choral ode *Das Meer* ('The Sea') by the Vienna Male Voice Choir.

One afternoon at about five o'clock, full of excited anticipation, we stepped inside the house (Hessgasse 7) and climbed up the stairs to the fourth floor. I rang the bell. Nothing moved! I rang again. Silence once again! My wife wanted to leave, but I stayed and waited tenaciously for another few minutes. Then I rang again.

After we had spent about ten to twelve minutes waiting in vain on the doorstep we finally heard shuffling steps and then a voice called out, 'Who's there?' – 'Nicodé.' With a cheerful 'Ah!' the door immediately opened and before us stood – Anton Bruckner in his shirt-sleeves, a candle held up high in his left hand. Warmly he invited us in, while apologizing, in an awkward, childlike manner, for his night-shirt. He led us through a dark room (the kitchen) and into his study (which ran parallel to the street). It was a large, very simply furnished room, in the middle an old piano with organ pedals and an organ bench. Next to this, near the window, stood an extremely small table which was only about ¾ metre long. A huge pile of scores had been piled up on top of it. On the corner of this table which was nearest to the piano there was a tiny triangular, empty space, which was covered in ink stains. This spot, on which you could just about fit a plate, was his desk! Most of the manuscripts which lay on top of it belonged to the Ninth Symphony, which he was working on at the time. After we had enquired about his health – Bruckner was suffering from a prolonged catarrhal cough, which had prevented him from attending the performance of my *Meer* – and I had told him about the success of his symphony which I had performed in Dresden, I asked him to give us a foretaste of his Ninth Symphony, which was in progress at the time. As with most orchestral composers, it was understandably difficult to persuade him to play his work on the piano; however, after initial resistance he agreed and played for us, on his old rickety piano and in his abrupt, almost choppy manner, sections of all the movements. Even if his playing itself did not immediately made a great impression, it nevertheless gave an inkling at some points of what the music was all about! I wouldn't swear to it, but I think he said to me then that if he did not live to complete a separate fourth movement, then he wished his *Te Deum* to be the last movement. Obviously pleased by my sympathetic interest, he gave me a signed picture of himself and then, looking innocently and lovingly at us, asked how long we had been married. 'Yes,' he said, 'I wish I could've managed it, but the women I loved didn't like me, and I didn't love the women who did like me.' Then his eyes began to gleam and you could see tear drops shining in them.

Finally he led us next door into his bedroom, which was just as big as his study. He pointed to the portraits of Beethoven and Wagner above his bed and said: 'They are my dear Masters.' In doing so he made a deferential, almost kneeling gesture towards them. He was proud, very proud in fact, of his beautiful, 'English' (he put particular emphasis on that word) brass bed, which he had recently been given by friends (I think he said his students). 'That's my luxury,' he said, pushing down on it repeatedly with both hands and saying with a beam, 'Look how you sink in.' That was Bruckner at his best! Before we left, he went over to a table which stood by the window and took out a handful of cigars from the cigar-cases which were piled up on it. He told us that he wasn't allowed to smoke, but that he received so many as presents from friends! We wished him a speedy recovery and many happy, productive years, to which he humbly replied: 'I'd love that, it all depends on Him up there!' Touched and moved by the simple kindness which we had experienced during our visit, we bade goodbye to the Master, who accompanied us to the door.

[Göllerich/Auer, 4/3, 144–7]

Could Bruckner really have recommended the *Te Deum* as a finale for the Ninth Symphony? Nicodé's uncertainty may strike some readers as significant. Apart from the enormous difference in character between the two works, there is no obvious thematic connection between the *Te Deum* and the three completed movements of the symphony (Bruckner finales normally bring back, or at least allude to, motifs from earlier movements, especially at the end); and it is difficult to imagine any composer as sensitive to long-term key relationships as Bruckner countenancing an arbitrary C major conclusion to a D minor symphony. Few modern Bruckner commentators seem disposed to take the idea seriously. But Nicodé is not the only writer who claims that the suggestion came from Bruckner himself.

CARL HRUBY

I saw Bruckner for the last time in front of the Alserkirche, just after High Mass – he had been playing the organ there at the special invitation of the choirmaster. I had not seen the Master for some while, so I was not prepared for the devastating change sickness had wrought upon his appearance. I was shaken, and had to make a special effort to maintain my self-control. Bruckner was tormented by presentiments of death – and by one thought in particular: that he would no longer be able to complete his Ninth Symphony. 'I've had a hard time with the Ninth. It's not the sort of thing you should try to do at my age and in my state of health. If I don't finish it, then my *Te Deum* should be used as the fourth movement. I've nearly finished three movements. This work belongs to the Good Lord!' We parted at the Schottentor. 'It's been an honour, Herr Professor!' – 'Adieu, dear Hruby!' – That was my last meeting with Anton Bruckner in this world.

[Hruby, 40–41]

Hugo Wolf's reported recollection of the dying Bruckner (p. 144) paints a comfortingly serene picture, but other accounts of the composer's last months tend to confirm Hruby's remark about his 'tormented' state of mind.

JOSEPH SCHALK

Vienna, 24 September 96
As regards Bruckner, I have very sad news. His mind is disintegrating, and the spectre of religious mania holds him ever faster in its grip. It makes a dreadful impression, and perhaps a quick end would be the best thing, as recovery is out of the question. He is, however, astonishingly tenacious of his bodily health. On my last visit (before the holidays), he exchanged a few words with me, then, ignoring me completely, he desperately recited the Lord's Prayer, loudly repeating each sentence. It was hard for me to hide my distress, so I crept away. At the moment I dare not visit him; I cannot bear it, it is too terrible. Admittedly, there will be better days, but they are impossible to predict.

[Schalk, *Briefe und Betrachtungen*, 65–6]

But these are brief impressions. By far the most extensive – and informative – account of Bruckner's last days is given by Dr Richard Heller. The remarks about the Ninth Symphony attributed to Bruckner are both thought-provoking and frustrating: if only Heller *had* been able to write down something of what he heard, or at least given a more detailed verbal description! Heller's report begins at the point when he took over from Dr Leopold Schrötter as Bruckner's private physician.

RICHARD HELLER

I got to know Bruckner in the winter of 1894, when he was recovering from a heavy attack of pleurisy; this, combined with an organic heart defect, had left him very weak and in poor spirits. Schrötter had handed Bruckner over to me and I visited him daily.

Early in the new year Bruckner moved to the Belvedere, where the Emperor had let him have the '*obere Stöckel*' ('the upper storey'), which was next to the Botanical Garden. The apartment was not big, but the room Bruckner lived in was quite spacious, with a view of the Belvedere garden through the three windows. Behind this were the other rooms: the kitchen, a living-room for his loyal housekeeper Kathi, and another room, further back, in which he kept all his souvenirs, ceremonial wreaths, ribbons, batons, etc.

His room was very simply furnished: a table with a big, leather armchair by the middle window; two boxes and a large chest of drawers, on which stood a big, black crucifix with a finely carved figure of Christ in ivory; left and right of this, two lamps with tall, wax candles; a very large, brass bed against the far wall; and in the middle of the room his old Bösendorfer grand, on which lay a perpetual jumble of music-paper and scores. The piano lid was usually covered with items of clothing which he wore according to mood or weather.

When I began my visits, there was also his great harmonium which stood in the corner of the room . . .

Remarkably, he recovered rather quickly during the year 1894, and he threw himself into composing as soon as he had moved to the Belvedere.

At that time, Bruckner was working on his Ninth Symphony, and since I am also musical, we talked about it from time to time.

Amongst other things he told me this, 'You see, I've already dedicated symphonies to two great royal persons, poor King Ludwig and our illustrious Emperor, for me the most exalted earthly ruler. And now I offer my last work to the King of Kings, the Dear Lord himself, and I hope He will grant me enough time to finish it, and that He will graciously accept it. For this reason I am going to bring back the Allelujah (he probably meant the "Te Deum") from the second movement* with full power in the finale, so that the symphony ends with a song of praise to the Dear Lord.'

Then he went over to the piano and played me parts of the symphony with shaking hands, but with undiminished accuracy and strength.

I have often regretted the fact that I cannot play or write down music after one hearing, because then I might have been able to give some idea of the end of the Ninth Symphony.

As he was so weak, I often begged him to write down the main ideas, but he could not be persuaded.

Page by page, he worked out the complete instrumentation, and I believe that some of his remarks indicate that in his mind he had drawn up a contract with his 'Dear Lord'. If He willed that the symphony, which was indeed to be a hymn of praise to God, should be finished, He should give Bruckner the time he needed for his task; if he died too soon and his musical offering was left incomplete, God had only himself to blame.

Religion was a primary force in the life of this great creative genius. He prayed regularly, and if his devotions sometimes took strange forms, they were still sincerely offered and deeply felt. It

*If Heller's remark is confusing at this point, so too is Max Auer's explanatory footnote: 'Trio of the Eighth Symphony with echoes of the *Te Deum*' [Kobald, 26]. Was Bruckner referring to the combination of the *Te Deum*'s quaver ostinato figure (C'''–G'' – G''–C'') with a transformation of the chorale theme from the Adagio third movement of the Ninth (Letter B), as can be seen in the sketches? The word 'Alleluia' can easily be made to fit the chorale's opening phrases in both versions, though anything less exultant than the Adagio chorale is hard to imagine. In his introduction to the printed sketches for the finale of the Ninth [*Anton Bruckner Gesamtausgabe: zu Band IX*], John Philips follows Auer's lead and suggests that '"Allelujah" can most convincingly be identified with a phrase from the Trio in the second movement of the Eighth (q.v., letter C).'

was impossible to disturb him when he knelt at prayer before his great crucifix, and so I often had the opportunity to hear what he said as I stood quietly with him in the room. There would be several 'Our Father's and 'Hail Mary's, and he would often conclude with a free prayer, for example: 'Dear God, let me soon be well again; you see, I need my health so that I can finish the Ninth', and so on. This last request was uttered somewhat impatiently; it was concluded with a threefold Amen, and on a few occasions, on the third Amen, he would slap his thighs with both hands, as if to say, 'If the Dear Lord doesn't hear me, then it's not my fault!'

He always prayed in a loud voice, and this led to an incident that put him in a bad mood for some time. As a rule, there was only a very small congregation for Mass at the little Belvedere Chapel, which was taken by an old, white-haired priest. Bruckner prayed out loud during the Mass, without thought for the priest or his surroundings – not surprisingly, given that his hearing was failing. One day, the priest asked him to keep his voice down, as it was making it hard for him to perform the holy office. The next time I saw him, he was in a terrible mood, repeating over and over again how insulting this was – no one could forbid a man to pray in the way he knew best. He insisted on going to the Emperor, and although we talked him out of it, he refused to return to the chapel; in future, he heard all his Sunday Masses in the city.

He was very concerned about his health, and every day one had to reassure him that nothing was the matter.

His title of Honorary Doctor at the Vienna University was of the greatest importance to him, and one always had to address him as 'Herr Doktor'.

Knowing that I played the piano and the harmonium, he told me one day that he would like to give me his harmonium, since he could no longer play it; working the pedals had become too much of an effort for him. I felt I could not allow him to give me something of such historic significance as the Bruckner Harmonium, so I thanked him, and told him that there might come a time when he needed it again. I related this to Schrötter, who accompanied me on my visit to Bruckner several days later. Schrötter, in his usual manner, suddenly brought the conversation round to the harmonium. Bruckner said that he had meant to give it to me, but that I would not take it, whereupon Schrötter promptly said, 'Well, then give it to me', which Bruckner immediately did. Generally speaking, Bruckner was of a mistrustful nature, and in his peasant-like way he would scent something suspicious in every tiny detail. It may also be significant that at that time he was seriously thinking of getting married. The only way to talk him out of this was to tell him that at the moment he was still too ill and weak, and that he must wait until he was restored to full health. Often he would sit out in the garden and feel reasonably well. On days when he was not well, his attitude towards his doctors would swing round and he would heap the bitterest reproaches on me. Usually these moods did not last long, and he would soon be imploring us to forgive him and not to desert him.

The summer of 1895 went by without his sickness reappearing, and by the autumn and winter he felt so well that he was able to attend a performance of his Symphony* by the Philharmonic.

Nevertheless, his mental alertness was in continual decline – not significantly, perhaps, but enough to be noticeable to those who saw him regularly. Slowly he became more and more infantile. One day he brought home a number of ladies' watches, which he had collected from a watchmaker in the city, to give to women as presents. Or he was constantly ordering new shoes – although the number he already owned was enormous. Cancelling these orders kept Kathi pretty busy. He had virtually no understanding of the value of money, as the following incident clearly shows. Although I expected nothing in return for my treatment of the Master (indeed I deemed it an honour to be able to do what I could for him) and he himself had said nothing on this subject, I was very surprised when one day, over a year after my first visit, he declared that he must pay me. With Kathi's help, I tried to dissuade him; but to no avail. He took out his purse, delved into it for quite a while, and at last put a fifty-guilder piece on the table. When Kathi saw this she cried out in horror, 'What do you think you're doing, Herr Doctor? For the time he's spent treating you!' Guiltily he stammered an apology and emptied the entire contents of his purse on to the table (about 300 to 400 guilders), pushing them towards

*'Fourth (Romantic) Symphony' [Auer's note].

me with the words, 'Yes, of course, of course. Take it, take it all – it's far too little.' It was only with some trouble and effort that I was able to persuade him to put the money back, and then only when I had assured him that I would present him with my bill.

At the beginning of July 1896, Bruckner suddenly fell ill. There were breathing difficulties and a serious onset of pneumonia which, given his old age and heart problems, made one fear for his life hourly. Schrötter, who now came with me every day, had given up hope. Bruckner's powerful constitution withstood even these attacks and, to our astonishment and joy, he recovered so quickly that he was soon able to walk about again. The photograph of Bruckner standing at the door of his house in his shirt-sleeves with Schrötter and me was taken at this time.

We have no portrait of Bruckner from his latter days, and as for suggesting that someone take his photograph, this was impossible, as he would have taken it as a sign of his approaching end. So we decided to photograph him without his knowing. Schrötter asked Fritz Ehrbar to take up the challenge. When Schrötter and I arrived, Bruckner was sitting in his armchair by the window (this was the eighth day of his illness!). Ehbar set up his equipment behind the door, so that all he had to do was open it and take Bruckner's picture. Perhaps the ever-mistrustful Bruckner suspected something, perhaps he had heard a noise behind the door – whatever the reason, he suddenly stood up and demanded that, since the day was so fine, we should go for a stroll. The camera was quickly hidden, whereupon he went out with Schrötter to the carriage, and Ehrbar was able to make the snapshot that is now in my possession. When we were alone, I suggested that he go to bed and sleep for a while, which he did, and it was then that Ehrbar took that extraordinary picture of 17 July 1896 – a picture which shows Bruckner as though in the final sleep of death . . .

Unfortunately Bruckner's mental health had also suffered during his last illness – each day, he became more childish and confused.

My wife often came with me on my visits; he was always pleased to see her and treated her with the greatest kindness.

Despite the decline of his mental powers, he continued to compose, and at times he was in such good spirits that he played *Ländler* for us.

On Sunday, 19 July, it rained heavily and was bitterly cold. All of a sudden, Bruckner insisted on going to church. His attendants could not allow this, and so he concluded that they wanted to deprive him of his freedom. When I arrived, he begged me to write out a certificate declaring that he would always have his freedom. He made me promise on my honour to do this, and I wrote the following:

In recognition of the outstanding achievements of Herr Professor Dr Anton Bruckner in the lifelong service to his art, it is hereby attested that, on the instant of his recovery, he should have and enjoy to the full complete freedom.

Vienna, 20 July 1896,

Dr Heller*

He himself dictated the words 'and enjoy to the full', and he repeated them several times. His joy over this – to use his own words – priceless document was indescribable: he insisted on kissing the hand of his 'life-saver', whereupon he embraced and kissed me repeatedly and said that there was only one way to thank me properly: he must write me a chorale. At the same time he promised me the finest cigars known to man – and whenever I went to see him, I had to take three cigars from the little box he always kept by him.

He began to work on the chorale the next day, writing down the theme on a fresh piece of music-paper that lay on the piano. Unfortunately I was unable to get hold of this personally priceless manuscript after his death, although his brother and Kathi confirmed that it belonged to me. Over the next few days he talked a lot about going out and taking a solitary stroll. He sent everyone out of the room so that he could tell me his plan in secret. As usual, he accompanied me to the door; and when I left for Obertraun on 15 August his physical health was much recovered.

Dr Sorgo stood in for me until my return on 15 September. I found that Bruckner's mental condition had declined much further, and the many corrections in the score made over the last year

*Heller writes what he terms an 'approximate' version of the 'certificate' in his reminiscence, and Auer adds the original as a footnote – I have used Auer's version.

showed that he found it harder to compose. He spent most of his time each day sitting in his armchair.

On 11 October there was a call for me at the clinic. I had gone out for a moment, and so it was half an hour later that I got to Bruckner and found him dead. He had died suddenly of a heart attack.

The poor man had hardly closed his eyes before the vultures fell on what he had left, and in an instant everything was signed and sealed.

[Kobald, 22–31, 33–5]

LIST OF SOURCES

Archiv für Musikwissenschaft, XXXIX Jahrgang, vol. 3, 1982, 1983

Auer, Max, *Anton Bruckner, sein Leben und Werke*, Vienna, 1932

Bachrich, Sigismund, *Aus verklungenen Zeiten, Erinnerungen eines alten Musikers*, Vienna, 1914

Decsey, Ernst, *Bruckner, Versuch eines Lebens*, Berlin, 1920

Eckstein, Friedrich, '*Alte unnennbare Tage*!', Vienna, Leipzig, and Zurich, 1936 [Eckstein]

Eckstein, Friedrich, *Erinnerungen an Anton Bruckner*, Vienna, 1923

A German Reader, Music in the Making, Hugo

Göllerich, August, and Auer, Max, *Anton Bruckner, Ein Lebens- und Schaffensbild*, 4 vols, Regensburg, 1922–37 [Göllerich/Auer]

Gräflinger, Franz, *Anton Bruckner, Bausteine zu seiner Lebensgesichte*, Munich, 1911 [Gräflinger]

Grassberger, Renate, and Partsch, Erich Wolfgang (eds), *Bruckner – skizziert*, Vienna, 1991

Heuberger, Richard, *Erinnerungen an Johannes Brahms*, Tutzing, 1971

Hruby, Carl, *Meine Erinnerungen an Anton Bruckner*, Vienna, 1901 [Hruby]

Kietz, Gustav, *Richard Wagner in den Jahren 1842–49 u. 1873–75, Erinnerungen*, Dresden, 1905

Klose, Friedrich, *Meine Lehrjarhre bei Bruckner*, Regensburg, 1927 [Klose]

Kobald, Karl (ed.), *In Memoriam Anton Bruckner*, Zurich, Vienna and Leipzig, 1924 [Kobald]

Kraus, Felix and Felicitas von, *Begegnungen mit Anton Bruckner, Johannes Brahms, Cosima Wagner*, Vienna, 1961 [Kraus]

Lochner, Louis, *Fritz Kreisler*, London, 1950

Mahler, Alma, *Erinnerungen und Briefe*, Amsterdam, 1940 [Alma Mahler]

Oberleithner, Max von, *Meine Erinnerungen an Anton Bruckner*, Regensburg [Oberleithner]

Schalk, Lili (ed.), *Franz Schalk, Briefe und Betrachtungen*, Vienna and Leipzig, 1935

Stradal, August, *Erinnerungen an Franz Liszt*, Bern and Leipzig, 1929

Wagner, Cosima, *Die Tagebücher*, Band II, Munich and Zurich, 1977

Weingartner, Felix, *Lebenserinnerungen* (second revised edition), Zurich, 1928

A German Reader, Music in the Making, Woodbridge, 1994

INDEX

Note: AB = Anton Bruckner
Bruckner's works are indexed alphabetically (under Mass, Symphony, etc.); all other works will be found under the name of their creator.